Lie Over Da

Aideen

BALLYHAY BOOKS

Published by Ballyhay Books,
an imprint of Laurel Cottage Ltd.
Donaghadee, N. Ireland 2004.
Copyrights Reserved.
© Text by Aideen D'Arcy 2004.
Printed by Colour Books Ltd..

ISBN 1 900935 36 8

*To Frank Doran, friend of many lifetimes,
who bought many an ice-cream, gave many
a lift and shared many a ghost story.*

*And to all the people of Dungannon, among
whom I grew up.*

Acknowledgments

I would like to thank the many people who helped this project through to fruition: best friend Isobel who, tired of my whinging that someone should write these stories down, made me do it; multi-talented writer, broadcaster, conservationist and fellow-Tyrone woman, Polly Devlin, herself a modern classic, whose warm and generous praise made me believe they had some merit; the Lutton, Fahy and Quinn families, who read the book in manuscript form and gave me so much encouragement; and above all, Kathleen Quinn and her son Ronan, whose friendship has enriched me since my Donaghmore Road days, and whose courage in the face of adversity takes my breath away.

Prologue
Maureen: A Memoir

Whilst sifting through the extensive memorabilia belonging to Maureen D'Arcy, with a view to compiling this memoir, it suddenly dawned on Aideen and me that we had been duped big time by her mother. This knowledge not only resulted in us hugging each other in uncontrolled and tearful hysteria, but also left the two of us with a feeling of justice and heartfelt relief. A few moments before we unearthed her secret, the task of attempting to unravel the life of this remarkable woman had seemed almost too much for us, but now our resolve had been strengthened by the smallest of facts and, to two girls bereft at the loss of a chum, it seemed at the time like Divine inspiration. The simple fact that she was older than she had ever cared to admit would not release her from Death's embrace, but it made us laugh to think she had cheated the old boy for longer than we had realised.

———— ∞ ————

Two years earlier as I had stood at her hospital bedside and watched her slip away into another world I had felt betrayed. How could this woman die, this Carmen Miranda of Dungannon with her sense of respectability at least as strong as Mrs. Morrell's in *Sons and Lovers*; this woman who laughed at adversity yet took Askit powders every four hours for the 'old arthur' with the same dedication as a dope addict, carefully opening the papers and deftly knocking the contents into a corner of the packet, then throwing the white powder to the back of her throat in a manner not unlike that of a cocaine victim snorting the powder through a rolled up paper note; surely she and Death had nothing to do with one another.

Maureen had always told us she would live as long as Happy Granny Snow and we had believed her because her love of life was so strong.

"A fortuneteller told me I would live to be as old as my grandmother Larkin," she insisted.

We accepted it as readily as the intelligence that she had hazel eyes.

Each moment had to be enjoyed, the best taken from it. If you got a mark on a new garment and were vexed or disappointed, Maureen would admonish you with, "Don't be silly child, a mere trifle, I'll fix that for you in no time", and she did. When Aideen would disappear off to bed, dropping with sleep, Maureen and I would light the cigarettes and put the kettle on and I would be seduced by her stories of people she had met and family tales. With her you felt invincible, she was the talisman; you could smoke your head off and never get any sleep and still your health would not suffer. I remember once asking Aideen why her mother would insist upon accompanying her on the smallest of journeys when it would be so much quicker to go on her own and Aideen responded,

"She thinks nothing will happen to me if She is there."

She had the child's capacity to enjoy the simplest of things. I remember driving to Kerry with her and she occupied herself by writing down the name of every town, village or hamlet that we passed through; months later she would produce the list and say,

"Och girls, do you remember The Pass of the Plumes?"

And yet she could make your troubles disappear, reduce your mountains to molehills and convince you that all would be 'as right as rain.'

No one could create an atmosphere like Maureen and it mattered not a jot if her canvas was your imagination or the interior of her front room because, long before the penchant for *Changing Rooms*, Maureen was a master of titivation. Christmases with Maureen were magical times that began on the eighth of December with the trimming of the tree and lasted until Twelfth Night when the decorations came down. I well remember her saying "Keep the feast till the feast day," but once it came, her enthusiasm knew no bounds. Sitting in the warm glow from the Christmas lights, delicious odours wafting from the kitchen and mixing with the scent from the candles, and always Christmas carols playing in the background, I felt myself close to heaven. She honoured all the traditions, spared no expense, swathed every nook and cranny with holly, tinsel and mistletoe, and every now and again would sit back and say,

"Sure there's no time like it."

Against such a background my love for this woman grew. Though a smoker all her life Maureen always exuded a beautiful aroma. She was like an Alchemist mixing potions; every time she ascended to her bedroom she would spray herself with a different scent, not from the Chanel or Balenciaga ranges but from Cookstown's bargain buckets and, as she aromatically wafted past you with a wink and a sashay she would say,

"That's the oul' coaxalorum."

A wordsmith of the highest order, Maureen would sit well into the wee small hours completing cryptic crosswords, or perhaps engage in embroidering a tablecloth, a frown of concentration on her face and the glasses chain dangling glamorously. All her life she considered herself plain – Posy was the beauty of the family – but everything she did, from smoking a cigarette to pleating her skirt before she sat down, was carried out with an air of elegance. She used a minimum of make-up, but to dispel the Campbell paleness she favoured a trace of rouge, which she referred to as "a rub of the relic". Every story she told us was "for your edification, girls"; she was our mentor, our mimic, our friend and protector.

When her own guard started to crack under her belief

that she had succumbed to cancer like her mother and Charlie before her, we were so caught up in the world she had created that we refused to believe the signs. Hadn't she always told us she would live until she was ninety-five? It was only in the previous year or so that Aideen had persuaded both her parents to collect their pensions. Her father had worked on past his retirement age and hadn't felt the need; Maureen simply would not admit to being old enough. When she died we estimated her age to be about seventy and had felt she was robbed of life. Two years later we were to discover that she was at least seventy-three if the War correspondence was anything to go by. To any reasonable person our reaction was bizarre; after all, what is a mere three years to someone who has no more left to them? But it made us laugh to think that she had fooled us for so long, that we had so willingly bought into her pretence, that she had maintained her ebullient youthfulness in the face of the inexorable march of time and that, in the end, given that she had existed for years on very little sleep and crammed every moment to the full, she had probably squeezed a few more years out of her allotted span and matched, if not exceeded, Happy Granny Snow.

Maureen like her brother Wilfred was a born entertainer; there just weren't enough hours in the day for them and both in life had appeared as indestructible as they were humorous because they shared a big spirit. They filled a room and belied their tiny physical frame by sheer force of personality. Neither showed any fear in approaching death but met their fate with a dignity that hitherto I had only read about. It is their essence that we hope to capture in these pages; their stories that we want to keep alive, but above all else we hope to remind ourselves that life is for living, life is for enjoying and that the smallest of dreams can come true.

ISSY (her number two daughter!)

REMEMBERING
MAUREEN CAMPBELL D'ARCY,
26 AUGUST 1920 (?) – 18 FEBRUARY 1994

Contents

My mother was in the corner shop one evening when in came Jimmy, all five feet nothing of him, sparse grey hair escaping from its carefully constructed comb-over, his fussy self-importance emanating from every shimmy of his would-be impressive gait. The assembled women allowed him to be served first, so that they could return to their conversation in peace.

"Imagine somebody married that," observed my mother after he had gone.

"You wouldn't have taken him, Maureen," remarked Kathleen, with a smile.

"No," replied my mother, "I don't collect curios."

But now, years later, remembering Maureen D'Arcy and everything that made her what she was, I realise that she did. She enjoyed eccentricity, relished 'characters' and welcomed difference. She got on with people to whom others gave a wide berth; "Sure, I take the crack out of them," she'd say. I never knew anyone to resist her blandishments. When she came to visit me as a student in Dublin, word went around: "Aideen's mother's down for the weekend," and the house would be full. She read the cards, strictly for fun, but she had such a way of setting the atmosphere and her own special turn of phrase while in this mode, that you always half-believed her. She never allowed us to prompt her in her readings, telling only what the cards were supposed to represent, but when a friend of mine confided that he would not sit his exams if she saw failure in the cards I had to warn her.

"For God's sake tell Brian something positive!"

"I foresee success for you here," she intoned. "Remember, it's the future I read. But much will depend upon the effort you make yourself; a little hard work will bring rich rewards."

Phew!

She was always ahead of her time. I was the only person in school who didn't have to smuggle out my miniskirt to change into when we got to the disco, for her belief that "You might as well be out of the world as out of the fashion," made her the envy of my friends.

She was a great champion of the young, "When I was your age, I wouldn't have seen you in my road," being her way of encouraging you to go for it; and she detested fogeyism. She hated the begrudgers, was generous with her time and with money and was always the last to leave a party or go to bed.

She was an excellent mimic, with the true comedian's knack of picking up on sayings and mannerisms that make each of us so distinguishable; and she loved being the centre of attention on a small scale, when holding court in her own house, but was oddly shy and lacking in self-confidence in the wider world.

She was a Nationalist in the true sense of the word, for she loved Northern Ireland, its scenery, music, sayings and folklore, and would often remark that if someone could get a spade and dig along the Border, cutting us adrift from the rest of Ireland, England and Europe, we would have the best wee country in the world. For above all she loved its people, saying they had the best sense of humour and knew how to laugh at themselves, a quality that has stood us in good stead these many years. Her brand of patriotism came from a deep-rooted sense of our own worth as a nation, and had more to do with the ideals of 1798 than the kind of perverted philosophy that holds to the belief that only one kind of religious or political view must be paramount, and so must destroy anything or anyone that doesn't follow slavishly in the same narrow furrow. I was brought up on a diet of ballad poetry and knew as much about Irish history when I went to school as I learned there. She was an old-fashioned Catholic, brought up among Protestants and would often remind me,

"Some of our best patriots were Presbyterian; never think religion has anything to do with it."

Her heroes included Robert Emmet and Henry Joy. Once her father and James Johnston, a pillar of the

Church of Ireland, went off to find the grave of Betsy Grey and rescue it from oblivion, in the days before anyone had enough sense to value national monuments. They cleared weeds and straightened the stone in a small tribute to the days when, as Thomas Davis reminds us, "In the cause of their country, the Irish agree." A pity more people didn't think like that.

She never met anyone who did not become a friend. It was always open season in our house and anyone who called at the door had to be invited in. When she met someone new she would say, like David Copperfield, "I enlarge my circle of acquaintance," and nothing pleased her more. As a child I hated going shopping with her, for she talked to everyone. In later life, crippled with arthritis, she still came with me on my many excursions and the development of the shopping centre was a boon to her, for I would leave her in a coffee dock in the central mall, while I browsed, and come back to find her tête-à-tête with a complete stranger, from which she would extract herself reluctantly, with promises to meet again. In the shops people would offer her a chair which she accepted graciously; a shop in Cookstown even kept an ashtray for her use.

Her ability to charm lay in a genuine liking for people, but she could be scathing in her criticisms and was a past master of the put-down. I remember walking in Castlewellan Park with my dog and my cousin's two Jack Russells when we met two elderly ladies. They regarded our canines with pinched noses and disapproving looks, evidently expecting them at any minute to rip their throats out or do something nasty in the flower beds (they were too well-trained for the latter and had too much taste for the former). Noticing my mother staring at them, they felt inclined to make some comment.

"Oh," said one, peevishly. "Dogs' day out?"

It was the opening from heaven. Maureen beamed at them.

"No," she replied, smiling sweetly. "Bitches'."

But deep down she always believed the best and, if once or twice in her life she was deceived, generally she amassed a legion of faithful friends and admirers. The thing she liked best in life was talking and as a consequence was a first-rate storyteller. Many of the people I celebrate in these pages are known to me personally; but just as many are known to me mainly, if not exclusively, through her stories of them. She loved their failings, their foibles, their oddities; and it should be remembered that none of her tales were told with malice. Gossip interested her not at all; she cared not where you lived or what your salary was; she would not have known what car you drove. But she loved humour, and, as everyone knows, the greatest humour always comes from the human condition.

So who was she, this doyen of raconteurs? She was born Maureen Campbell, second child of a prosperous farming family in Ballymulderg, a townland of The Loup outside Magherafelt, on the twenty-sixth of August, in or around 1920. The doctor who delivered her was drunk, which led him, so she said, to put the wrong year on her birth certificate; but certain other documents to which he cannot have had access have dates which have clearly been tampered with, so I cannot vouch for the veracity of this story! Her refusal to admit her age I once found irritating, later funny; now I see that it was her way of refusing to grow old and as such wasn't a bad idea at all.

The house where she grew up was a solid farmhouse of typical Ulster design, with neat outhouses surrounded by fertile fields. There was a small orchard with a stream running through it and a spring well from which they drew drinking water. The garden had been lovingly and skilfully laid out by her mother, Mary (Minnie) Larkin, with box hedges, cherry and beech trees and seats cut into the banks. Minnie's cousin Tom O'Brien used to stand up in the trap as he passed the gates to admire it from the end of the long loanin that led up to the front door. There was a moss a mile or so away where they cut turf and a magical place known as The Rock, a hidden enclosure full of whins where a child could get lost for many a long summer's day, or an elder brother could have his first taste of a cigarette.

Among the animals was a big work horse called Dick, who adored my grandfather; sheep, whose lambs were forbidden to be petted, for their departure always caused tears; chickens, with geese and turkeys at Christmas; and of course dairy cows. Great-grandmother Larkin, 'Ma', known to the neighbours as 'Happy Granny Snow' because of her white hair and great age, shared their abode, along with her other daughter, Brigid, two years younger than Minnie. An accomplished musician, Brigid would bring her accordion out into the fields in the evenings, while the cows would amble down to the hedgerow to stand and listen.

Minnie, who would become my grandmother, married Wilfred Campbell from Magherafelt, who, though born a 'townie', took to country life like a natural, and to family life, and soon there were four wee ones to augment the household.

Charlie, the first-born, went to the village school where he was taught by Mrs. O'Kane, a cousin of his mother's. The twenty or so pupils sat in a semi-circle around a turf fire and she taught them all, from infant to school-leaver, instilling in them a love of learning, sound principles and a good basic education. My mother, though too young to start, was sent along to swell numbers when there was a threat of closure due to falling enrolment, and to the day she died could quote pieces of poetry, capital cities or Irish mountain ranges with the best of them.

But like all idylls, this one was destined to end. When Aunt Brigid married and produced four children of her own, the farm could not support everyone. Ma had willed it to my grandmother with an entail which directed that it should pass to Charlie after her death, but my grandmother persuaded her to change her will, leaving Brigid the farm and herself a sum of money, for she and her husband had plans to strike out on their own. He would go to America for a year or two while she would set up in business with his brother, Tom, in a new location, with Granny investing her share of the inheritance in the venture. They decided upon a boot and shoe shop, for my great-grandfather Campbell was the owner of a small factory of cordwainers, and Tom had some expertise in this area. The old man was a typical Edwardian father, who ruled his family with a rod of iron, and when Wilfred asked him to finance his studies to enable him to become a chemist, he refused, saying that as eldest son, he was expected to follow him into the business. But Wilfred was strong-willed and so the task fell to Tom. Needless to add, Wilfred and his father parted on bad terms and no reconciliation ever took place. When, in his will, Campbell senior left my grandfather a sum of money, he was already in the States and he wrote home to his brother,

"So it seems that my father has bequeathed me some money. I am sorry that he did not see fit to give it to me at a time in my life when it would have been of value to me. When death had to wrest his filthy lucre from him I want none of it; but if it should be useful to my wife and children I beg that you will see it is made over to them."

They never saw a penny of it.

My grandfather went to America and my grandmother came to Dungannon c. 1925, with her four young children, Wilfred junior only four months old, and premises were found in Irish Street. But a gentleman's agreement, described by one solicitor as 'the curse of Ireland', is, as Sam Goldwyn might have said, not worth the paper it's written on, and soon problems arose. Tom disliked the children, saying they 'spoiled the tone of the place'; the situation became untenable, and my grandfather counselled a move, to temporary accommodation, until he would come home and sort things out. But weeks became months and time slipped by, and before long he had been diagnosed with a malignant brain tumour and died in Secauses, New Jersey, leaving a widow with no income, no business and a family to support.

In later years, I asked my mother,

"How *did* Granny manage?" and she replied,

"I have no idea."

She never complained and she never whinged and we can only guess at the anguish she must have suffered, not only at the loss of her partner, but at the loss of everything she owned, and at finding herself at one minute the daughter of a well-off farmer, the next a woman of business, and the next a widow wondering where the next meal was coming from. But she did manage and she earned the respect and admiration of all who knew her. She was a remarkable woman, of great strength of character and great wisdom; and most amazing of all, she had no bitterness in her nature and no rancour against those whose action, or in some cases, inaction, had left her where she was.

So Maureen Campbell came to Dungannon; but she always regarded herself as a Derry woman, carefully cultivating the remnants of the Derry lilt in her accent and cheering for Derry in football matches. But she came to love Dungannon and its characters almost as much as she loved her place of birth, to which they were able to return during school holidays, and I hope to catch something of their charm in these random reminiscences. From the man in The Loup who used to walk naked around the lanes wielding a cut-throat razor, and speel up a telegraph pole if anyone accosted him, to Willie Holland, placid and soft-spoken, who owned the worst-natured bull in County Derry, and who had discovered that the only way to get the animal into its stall after it had been on the razzle was to run in front of it and allow it to charge him, rigging up an escape hatch in the byre through which he could pass and the bull could not, allowing him to reach in, grab its nose ring and so tether it; from the Dungannon woman whose twenty-year absence from the town was matter-of-factly attributed to the fairies, to the housekeeper who persisted in removing the mantles from the gas-lamps every day, convinced that they were the work of a particularly malevolent breed of spider, Maureen loved and valued them all, and taught me to do the same.

If you recognise anyone in the following pages, know that the tales were told with affection rather than malice; as my mother said,

"Sure, we're only taking the crack out of them."

Curses Like Chickens

"We have loved her in life,
let us not forget her in death."

In Fond and Loving
Memory of
Anna Lowe
Liskittle House,
Stewartstown,
Who died on
27th May, 1947
Aged 18 years
R.I.P.

My Jesus, Pardon and
Mercy, through the merits of
Thy Sacred Wounds. — 300
days.

My grandmother, Mary Josephine Larkin, usually called Minnie, was the elder daughter of John and Britta (Brigid) Larkin and sister of Brigid.

Her paternal grandfather, John senior, being a man of substance and the father of four sons, decided to settle them all on farms in the area so, as land became available, he would buy it up providing, over the course of time, comfortable livings for each of them. When it came to John junior, there was no suitable place, but then word went out that a neighbour man was in debt and must sell and go to America. Harry himself came and offered the sale to Larkin and a deal was struck, but Ireland has always had her share of begrudgers and he was no exception. Although he was forced to sell through ill-luck or bad management, he hated the idea that another family would have his farm, so he laid a curse on the buyer. Old Sarah Milligan, the local wise woman and unofficial midwife for the parish, was returning home late from a confinement, on foot as was customary, when she saw Harry up in The Rock, building a fire of stones, the sure sign of a curse being set. She stole closer to listen. She heard him curse the name of Larkin and wish that it would die out of Ballymulderg. My grandmother had sixty-four first cousins scattered throughout the surrounding townlands, many of them male; her father alone produced only female issue, both of whom bore sons, but without the Larkin surname. Aunt Brigid named her youngest son Desmond Larkin O'Connell, but at time of writing he is a man in middle age, unmarried and without issue; none of his siblings have any family. When he dies, not only the name, but also the family of Larkin, will have quitted Ballymulderg forever.

There is a saying that 'curses, like chickens, come home to roost', and it may be so, but ill will towards another human being can have a most inimical effect on the object of it. The Larkin family had for generations been friendly with the Johnstons, an association that has persisted to the present day. As a boy, my uncle Charlie would spend long days with James, working on the farm, making hay, foddering cattle, while James's sister Annie, a noted cook and baker, would toil away preparing food for the family and their hired hands. In the days before

EU regulations, it was her practice to put things like apple tarts out on the window sill to cool, and it was a poor day if the boys didn't sample one or two titbits from Annie's morning's work. As the families grew up and settled down, it happened that John Johnston was on the look-out for land to build on, and in an uncanny echo of the situation facing my great-great-grandfather, a place became available when the owner drank himself out of house, land and credit, and selling-up was the only option. But he hated the Johnstons, and would not sell to them; it was only after he died that the place came into John's possession.

Soon a new bungalow graced the site, and John and his young wife moved in. I remember being shown around the house while it was still under construction, or rather tagging along with the adults who were infinitely more interested in kitchen layout, heating systems and roof pitch than I was. It was a beautiful summer's day, not a cloud in the sky, and my cousin Frank and I were more curious to see where the lane went, or if there might be kittens in the barn. I also remember that when we came home, my uncle Charlie said to my father,

"What did you think of the house, Pat?" to which he replied,

"I didn't like it one bit."

Here I pricked up my ears, for I could sense something unsaid.

"You wouldn't like to say a bit more?" pursued Charlie in that laconic way he had which concealed a keen intelligence and sharp wit.

My father looked at him.

"Would I be right in thinking we're on the same wavelength?" he asked, for they usually were, being firm friends before my mother embarked upon the course of action that made them brothers-in-law.

"Aye."

"I didn't like the feel of it," my father admitted. "I can't say why, but it didn't feel right."

"No," said Charlie. "It didn't feel right. There's something very much 'not right' about that place, and I wouldn't live in it for a pension."

I promptly forgot about the conversation in the way that children do, until several months later when a letter came from my mother's Aunt Brigid. Because I was an only child I was privy to most of the things that were discussed in the house, for I had learned from an early age that if I buried my head in a book and curled up in the corner of the big red Rexene couch that stood under the jamb window, people tended to forget I was there. Unfortunately, I often became engrossed in the book I had taken up as camouflage and missed things, but not on this occasion.

"And she says," went on my mother, "that John Johnston can't live in the house."

John's account went something like this. For the first few weeks, all went well. The house was decorated, furniture chosen, visitors came to admire, and life went on. Then one night he was awakened by an unmerciful racket out in the farmyard. He leapt up at once and rushed out to check on the animals but, although they were clearly distressed, there was nothing to account for it. The next night a repeat performance, and this time it occurred to him that it was probably local youths playing tricks on the newly weds, as was their wont in country areas, and he tried to ignore it. But it continued for longer than was acceptable, and again he went outside intending to give as good as he got should he catch anyone, but as soon as he got outside the noise ceased, only to start again *inside the house*. Now John was a man of the land, strong and dependable, not given to flights of fancy, but when this disturbance was repeated night after night, he began to think he was going crazy or someone seriously had a grudge against him.

He told my Aunt Brigid that he took to sleeping with a loaded shotgun at his bedside, but he finally decided to get help.

"I woke one night," he said, "with the certain knowledge that something or someone was standing over me in the bed, and that it meant me no good."

So he and his wife packed up and went to stay with friends, until, over the next few days, both their own minister and Fr. Quigley, parish priest at The Loup and a cousin of my mother's, had visited the house. No one ever spoke of the incidents again, and John and his family dwelt their day in the house, and as far as I know, their family are in it still.

When Charlie was told the story, his response was immediate.

"Harry Mallon never wanted a Johnston in his place," he said. "I'm not surprised he tried to drive John out."

Curses of course, were not confined to humans, and animals could also be afflicted. A common diagnosis for ailments for which there was no obvious explanation, was that the animal was 'blinked'; another way of saying it had been blighted with the evil eye.

There was a prize heifer at Ballymulderg who always threw a good calf, and this particular year was no exception. Now, as everyone knows, a heifer's milk is at its best after calving, but in this case the milk was undrinkable. Local experts, and in the last resort the vet, professed themselves puzzled, for the cow had no sign of any disease. Then she began to fade and for no apparent reason seemed to be dying. At this point enter Sarah Milligan.

"Ach, daughter," she said to my grandmother, "someone has blinked her."

So what could be done? The cure, Sarah assured them, was to tie a bit of red flannel around the animal's leg or neck and this would divert the ill wishing. Now my grandmother was a woman of great scepticism where superstition was concerned, but she also was wise enough to respect what she did not understand and to know when she was beaten. So the red flannel was produced and tied to the cow; and within a week she had begun to mend, and her milk was as sweet as ever.

Then again, curses did not always have a human provenance, and any interference with the fairy folk could result in extreme retribution.

There are two incidents in my family, which have always been regarded as a brush with the fairy kingdom, and if they carry no proof, at least they beg the question.

Ned Larkin was a cousin of my grandmother's who lived in a fine old farmhouse at a bend in the road that was always known as Ned's Turn. It was a long, low, two-storey house with a double staircase, and the usual outhouses. In common with most farming families of the time, Ned kept a servant girl and several men to work on the land.

There was a curious copse on Ned's land which everyone called The Leachan. It was a prime spot for the gathering of hazel nuts in the autumn but most unusually, the ground in this wooded place was covered in dozens of tiny mounds like miniature drumlins. One day Ned announced his intention of 'stubbing' it, uprooting the trees and undergrowth, and preparing it for cultivation. The land was good on his farm and another field would add to his pasturage or yield a crop. There was some resistance on the part of his men, for everyone felt the spell of The Leachan and believed, though they knew not why, that it should be left alone. But Ned pressed on, as a man with no time for nonsense will, and if on the first day one of his horses went lame, and a week later Atty McQuillan broke his leg at the work, sure it was only coincidence.

The women's work went on as usual and Ned's wife set the servant girl to washing blankets as the year was approaching the summer.

One night Ned awoke with a bad stomach. There was nothing unusual in this; for years he had suffered from an ulcer, and kept a bottle of medicine to hand in the kitchen cupboard and, as he always did, he went down to take some. He always kept it in the same place and never bothered to measure it; a mouthful would do the trick. But as soon as he swallowed it he recognised his dreadful, tragic error. He had inadvertently lifted the ammonia the servant girl had been using to wash the blankets!

When the alarm was raised, Ned's wife sent at once for my grandfather, the nearest neighbour. He set off on his bicycle to Magherafelt for the doctor, knowing in his heart it would be too late. In the days before phones, faxes and fast cars, a distance of a few miles often made the difference between life and death. But for Ned it was not an issue; he walked the floor in agony before succumbing to the fatal dose he had taken; the doctor said it burned from the moment he swallowed it.

The death of the man of the house made a huge difference in days past. The house was sold, passing out of the family altogether, and, of course, work on The Leachan ceased. The last time I saw it a few years ago, the hazel trees had reclaimed it. Oddly enough, in the course of time the house came back into the Larkin family, through the marriage of my mother's cousin to a man who had inherited it from a distant relative.

The tale intrigued me. Was there a force at work to stop Ned's clearance of the site? I discovered many years later that in Irish, the word 'leacha' can be used to describe virgin soil that has never been ploughed. It can also mean 'gravestone'.

Dan Lowe was another man who might have learned from Ned's tale, had he been of that frame of mind.

He was the husband of my great-aunt Maggie, the father of six boys and one much-loved daughter, Anna. He called her 'the wee beggar-woman from Stewartstown' (their nearest town), for she could persuade him to anything she set her mind to, like the time she cajoled him into letting her ride a half-broken colt into the town to buy her father a plug of tobacco. She returned, breathless and windswept, but none the worse for her madcap jaunt. She was a great favourite in the family circle, for she was not spoilt, and had a sunny nature and happy disposition; and was as much loved by her brothers as by her parents.

Dan farmed a huge acreage in County Tyrone, but one field had never been cultivated – the one with the thorn tree in the middle of it.

From time immemorial the Irish have cherished a fearful respect for the thorn tree, regarding one that stands alone – the 'lone bush' – as in some way special to the fairies. Our history, folklore and music are full of references to this belief, and it is said that one of the runways at Shannon airport was redirected during construction when the workers refused to uproot a fairy thorn. What the origin of this belief is I don't know; but curiously, it is a belief found throughout Africa where people believe that a solitary tree is the dwelling-place of an earth spirit and should not be moved. If removal is essential, the spirit must be propitiated with offerings. We all know the fairies dance around such a tree, but surely they would not react so violently if that were all it meant to them?

Maggie Lowe was one who treated the old ways with respect, and she was vehemently opposed to her husband's plan to dig out the tree, arguing that it was doing no harm, and in any case,

"They say if you offend the fairies they'll destroy something you value."

But Dan was adamant, perhaps because he wanted the field, or perhaps out of bravado, or a genuine sense of the foolishness of such views. And no one was hurt, no machinery failed, and the field was ploughed and sown, and in the autumn yielded its crop.

On the following St Patrick's Day Anna came to visit my grandmother. It was a cold, sleety day, one of the many on which our patron saint failed to turn up the sunny side of the stone. Anna sat by the fire with her feet on a stool and complained that she could not get heat into her; she hadn't felt well for a while, she said, she must be taking the cold. But what Anna sickened from, the doctors could not determine. She became progressively weaker and, though Dan spared no expense and called in specialist after specialist, they were baffled. Finally, one doctor obtained news from America of a wonder drug which might help reverse the decline. It was ordered and procured, but Anna's doctors were afraid to use it since it was unknown to medicine on this side of the Atlantic, and they had no time to test it. And so Anna died at eighteen years of age, with her life in front of her and everything to live for, thereby robbing her father of the one thing he valued above all others. The final diagnosis was given as 'a germ in the bloodstream'; today we might say leukaemia, or a rogue virus.

The night before Anna's funeral, my aunt Mona dreamt of being in a room containing a wrought-iron bed on which was a rolled-up mattress, but no bedding. In the corner of a deep window recess was a pile of books and a silver cross and chain hanging from a nail in the wall. She crossed to the window and looked down upon an unfamiliar yard. The next morning upon arrival at Lowe's, Dan asked my grandmother to go to Maggie. Some time later Mona went in search of them. Although she had visited the family often, she had never been further than the sitting room and, as it was a large and rambling house, she was at a loss as to where she might find them. Soon the sound of voices reached her and following the sound she found herself in a small back bedroom, the very same room she had seen in her dream, looking down on part of the yard invisible from the ground floor. As she entered she heard Maggie say,

"It's probably nothing but superstition, Minnie, but I wish he had left the fairy tree alone."

Ballymulderg

My mother's formative years were spent in the townland of Ballymulderg outside Magherafelt, in the parish of The Loup. Like many of our townlands, it no longer exists; now there is Mulderg Road, surrounded by Ballyriff Road, Oaklea Road and all the rest of those pointless appellations that tell us nothing about the topography or history of the place we call home. Like John Hewitt, I would take my stand by the Northern names, were I allowed to. I would stand on the ridge of the cuckoo, visit the land division of the cranes; climb the hill of the boasting to the pool of the cold summit, or walk in the wood of the wild cotton – if I was let. But today I drive through Ashley Close, leading to Ashley Grove, leading to Ashley Crescent, leading to yet another meaningless set of titles, which neither define nor describe the places they are attached to. And as the names described the places, so the places formed the people; my mother was a Ballymulderg woman, different from those who came from Corneyharvey or the Black Quarter and a world apart from the inhabitants of the Long Town (Cookstown) where in later years she loved to shop.

Everyone in Ballymulderg farmed and in my grandmother's day, when no one had very much more than his neighbour, they helped each other out whenever the occasion demanded it. At harvest time, flax-pulling, lambing, all the neighbours went first to one house, then to the next in a custom known as 'morrowing', until all the work was done; then they had a big night, the biggest barn usually the preferred location. One family of cousins, the Conwells, boasted seven strong sons who used to walk to each morrowing venue preceded by a fifer, who would wait until the day's work was over and then solemnly fife them home again. They knew how to work and how to laugh and they had a real sense of community. The Larkin family was the only Catholic family in the townland, but they lived through rebellion and civil war, the Black and Tans and the B-men, without threat or injury, because of their good neighbours. The story is told of my great-grandmother coming into the house one day saying,

"You may say your prayers, childer, for Scullionstown was burnt out last night."

Scullionstown was a small Catholic enclave a few miles away where all the families came of the same extended clan; hence the nickname. But my family kept the roof over their heads, and it later emerged that a neighbour man had put the word out that if anything were to happen to Mrs. Larkin, he and a few more would be looking for answers. And all this in spite of the fact that my grandmother's first cousin had fought for an Irish Republic, opposed the Treaty and been shot by the armies of the Free State, having been arrested in Donegal by a patrol led by his own cousin, a Major Morris, who saw things a bit differently.

Brigadier General Sean Larkin (Johnny) was a young man with a dream – of an Ireland independent of any other sovereign state wherein all men could live as equals – for which he was prepared to pay the ultimate price. Family lore relates that while in prison awaiting execution he was offered a reprieve if he renounced his stance and transferred his allegiance to the pro-Treaty camp. This he was reluctant to do, but he wrote home to his mother saying that if she wished it, he would do it for her sake. She wrote back saying, "Never give in, John." And so, aged twenty-seven, he went to face the firing squad on a cold March morning in 1923 along with three companions who had been arrested with him – Tim O'Sullivan, Daniel Enright and Charlie Daly. And though in later years his name has been used by those whose ideals are not as clear or unselfish as his, he remains to his family a shining example of a man with a vision of a better society whose idealism, perhaps, would have sat ill with the harsh realities of life in those trouble times, but who always hoped that one day all Ulstermen would see themselves as brothers. My mother was only a toddler when Johnny died, but she remembers her mother's grief at the death of her handsome young kinsman, described by all who knew him as big Jack Larkin, a man of quiet courtesy, unfailing good humour and strict honesty. His comrades recall a man who acted from conviction and was therefore unshakeable, an upholder of temperance and good conduct. And yet there was none in the family who condemned Morris; like Johnny they deplored what he called "this terrible and unfortunate Civil War", and wished only for reconciliation.

A touching story from his childhood tells of the occasion when, being sent to the shoemaker for a pair of shoes for Confirmation, he came back the proud possessor of a pair of heavily nailed boots; many years later my uncle Wilf did the very same thing, though it is unlikely he knew of Johnny's example. They were so noisy that my mother and Mona refused to let Wilf accompany them to Mass, for he enjoyed the clatter he made on the tiled floor and the embarrassment it caused to them. But my grandmother insisted, for she knew he wouldn't go on his own, and they extracted a promise of good behaviour from him in return for which he was allowed to make up one of their party. The girls swept into church full of the importance of teenagers with Wilf behind as quiet as a mouse; half-way up the aisle Mona nudged my mother and gestured over her shoulder; Wilf was making his progress up the aisle on all fours, much to the amusement of the congregation.

———— ⊗ ————

But friendship and mutual respect was stronger than anything which might have differentiated the families in Ballymulderg and on St Paddy's night the Larkins gave a party to which everyone came, dancing to the early morning with songs and stories and mighty crack. On the eleventh of July the Larkins went to Steel's or Waterson's or Johnston's in their turn and no one saw anything odd in that. Every eleventh night also, Sam Patterson would bring a Gladstone bag full of sovereigns down to Larkins for safe-keeping while he was away at the Twelfth and he would collect it again on the thirteenth when he had recovered sufficiently to do so.

Much is said today of how liberal society has become. We live in an anything goes world where it's fine to be yourself – or do we? It seems to me as if people were far more tolerant years ago. True, having a baby out of wedlock would have been frowned upon and nobody would have understood the concept of a gay icon, but oddness and eccentricity in character was accepted without question. You might have heard someone described as 'a bit odd', but he or she was not ostracised or castigated because of it.

Witness the said Sam Patterson. A well-to-do farmer with a fine house and a good bit of land, Sam had a penchant for acquiring other people's property by fair means or foul. He was, in fact, a kleptomaniac, but no one in Ballymulderg knew that word, or would have used it if they had. But everyone knew that Sam was not a criminal, you just had to keep an eye on him. My aunt Brigid would call the youngsters about her.

"Go and lift anything that's lying about, like a good child; Sam'll be down later".

For Sam also did odd jobs for all the neighbours, putting up a fence here or there, mending gates and so on, not for recompense, just because he was handy. Bob Steel asked him to fix a fence for him as soon as he could get into Magherafelt to get the wire.

"Ach sure I'll sort you out a wee bit myself," Sam assured him.

Days later Bob realised Sam had simply removed the wire from a neighbour's field, leaving him to go looking for someone to mend a bit of fence for him!

In those days all ploughing was done with horses and before a field could be ploughed ready for sowing it had to be opened with a smaller ploughshare.

"Dammit," says Dan O'Connell one day, "I'm damned if I can find the wee opening plough."

"Try Sam," advised aunt Brigid dryly.

Dan went up to Sam's place and asked for the loan of an opening plough.

"Come on down to the shed, son, and help yourself," Sam offered, escorting Dan into a shed laid out like a hardware store, in one corner of which was the best selection of opening ploughs you'd see in a day's walking, among them, Dan's own. Naturally nothing was said. Dan took the plough home with many thanks and made sure to lock it securely away once its work was done. The same Dan was coming home late from his ceilidh one night, walking, naturally, when he saw on the horizon an impossibly tall shape, man-like but at least ten feet tall. Not one of a nervous disposition, he nonetheless stood into the ditch until he could get a better view. But it was only Sam, all six foot of him, going home with a wheelbarrow that he had spotted earlier in the day and had come back for under cover of darkness. He was carrying it on his shoulders, holding the handles in front of his chest; it was the front wheel that gave the illusion of a human head and had made Dan stop in his tracks. Sam was unabashed, Dan uncritical.

"Goodnight son," said Sam as he drew level.

"Goodnight Sam," said Dan, as he passed on his way.

Madness in all its forms was well represented in the townland. There was Tom Foster, shell-shocked from his experiences in the First World War and mad enough to begin with. He could be seen most days with a billhook in one hand and a knife in the other, swinging them round and round his head, walking the fields and shouting orders to his imagined troops. He spoke much about Hill 60, and would ask anyone he met,

"Who's your model? Mine's O'Leary," – a throwback to his old life as an army man.

His favourite trick was to run down his lane stark naked with a cutthroat razor in his hand, and speel up a telegraph pole at the bottom of the loanin. My grandfather, from whom my mother inherited her love of the bizarre, often enjoyed a conversation with Tom, for there were times when he was completely normal and could discourse on any subject. He noticed that suddenly, sometimes in mid-sentence, Tom would pass his hand over his forehead as if he had a headache starting, and next moment would be completely irrational. This knowledge did not prevent Grandfather Wilfred from accepting an invitation to visit Tom in his own home, but he went thinking that Tom's father, Tom senior, would be in the house too and therefore able to keep an eye on the proceedings. But the younger Tom was alone. Despite serious misgivings, my grandfather enjoyed a fascinating conversation with Tom, who was reassuringly rational, apart from saying,

"My father, the old fool, doesn't remember that I was at school with both him and my mother."

But he explained to my grandfather that there were cables keeping him down from Heaven and these he had to try to cut through – hence the billhook, one supposes.

"Why don't you come down and visit me?" invited my grandfather, as he took his leave.

"I would, Wilfred, but it's very hard for me. I have to pass through a horse and then through a dog to get to where you live. But I'll try."

Wilfred let this pass, but weeks later came upon the spectacle of Tom bathing naked in a stream. As he watched, he jumped out and ran across a field to a large haystack, running round and round it to dry off and shaking himself, as a dog might. Did he imagine some sort of transmigration for himself? We can only guess. But months later he came to Johnston's, who lived across the road from Larkin's and asked for the boss.

"He's not in," replied Mrs. Johnston, terrified, for

———— ∞ ————

Tom was a man of no mean stature and his madness was no secret.

"Never mind," said Tom. "Tell him a man with a loaf of bread in one pocket and a couple of herrings in the other called to see him and will call again. But don't call with me, for he'll only find Tom in the spirit; Tom in the flesh will be somewhere else."

We can only assume it was my grandfather he was looking for, but sadly he never made the journey again. The powers that be deemed it wiser for him to be removed to Derry asylum, but it took several men to overpower him and get him into the ambulance the day they came for him. What a tragedy that a man of the highest intelligence in his saner moments should suffer so; and yet, perhaps it turned out all right for him. He told my grandfather that he stood on Hill 60 while the bullets were flying round him knowing he was invincible,

"Because that was only Tom in the spirit. Tom in the flesh was safe at home."

Maybe it was only Tom in the flesh that made that sad trip to Gransha, while Tom in the spirit continued to run wild in the woods like the noble savage, as free as nature first made man.

When my mother was little, a newcomer moved into the area, renting a small house, known as a 'cotter house' from one of the farmers. She was known as Miss Hall. No one knew where she came from or anything about her, but in the manner of children everywhere the young bucks of the neighbourhood soon discovered that if they shouted 'Up Davy!' she would quite literally go mad, screaming and shouting and ready to kill. She was very well spoken and knew how to make her point. She was walking one day near the Woods Church where a wedding was in progress. As the guests were arriving, a local smart-alec drove his car quite close to her, forcing her to jump into the ditch. When he came out of the church she had plastered a notice across his windscreen:

EZ murder car –
attends weddings to provide victims for funerals.

(Anyone with an aptitude for automobile history can work out in what year Derry cars were registered with the letters EZ!)

She came to Joe O'Connell, aunt Brigid's husband, for help in filling in her census form.

"I'll have to ask you some personal questions, Miss Hall," he explained. She didn't bat an eyelid at date of birth or anything else until he came to religion. She went into peals of laughter.

"Mr O'Connell, I'm surprised at you! Don't you know I belong to the Old Boy himself?"

Even after this disclosure, my mother and her cousins - the O'Connell girls, Maureen and Frances – were still sent up with small gifts of milk or butter or fresh-made bread, for Miss Hall was not well off. They were well warned not to go in, for they were always invited, but curiosity got the better of them one day and in they went. They were not prepared for the fact that she locked the door behind them and put the key in her pocket. The place was in almost total darkness, for she had shuttered all the windows. There was a cheerful enough fire burning in one corner of the room, though the fire-grate itself was empty. A pile of stones occupied the space beside the front door. These, she explained, were used to deter the intruders who sometimes threatened her;

"And these," she said, drawing from her pocket a wicked-looking pair of scissors, "are to poke out the eyes of anyone who looks through my keyhole."

"We'd better go," said the girls at this juncture.

"Before you do," said their hostess, "Let me show you where Tarzan and the apes feed."

She led them to the other ground-floor room which was also locked, and bade them look through the keyhole. Inside was a long wooden table scattered with crumbs and the remains of foodstuffs, indistinguishable and indescribable.

"They come every day," she assured them, before leading them back to the front door without further ado, and opening it, with many expressions of thanks for themselves and for the family. They had barely reached the end of the short garden path when a shout of "Up Davy!'" came from the other side of the low boundary wall; Wilfred junior and Dan O'Connell were lying in ambush. Miss Hall reacted as she always did, but the girls didn't stay to see the full performance; the account given by the boys before they were caught and chastised by their respective mothers was graphic enough.

———— ∞ ————

Of course it would be a gross distortion to suggest that madness was the only trait displayed by my mother's neighbours, or that it was peculiar to that area. Eccentricity played its part too. Another family, let's call them the Mitchells, were renowned for two things: lack of intelligence and lack of hygiene, so much so that to this day, any member of my family coming into the house and finding it like a dunderin-in will shake their head and say, "The Mitchells."

They too owned a good bit of land both in Ballymulderg and neighbouring townlands. One day my grandfather met them coming home and enquired what they had been doing all day.

"Building a wall," said George.

"That's a terrible dangerous thing to do," said Wilfred, "sure you could have built one of yiz into it. Are you sure all five of you are here?"

And so the count began; George could only account for four, as could Tom; John said they were both stupid, but when he made his tally, all he could see were four brothers. My grandfather left them to it, arguing about the problem and its implications, each one consistently forgetting to include himself in the count. My mother always said they went back and pulled the wall down, but never figured out where the missing brother had gone to, but I strongly suspect that this was an embellishment of her own.

In the army of the intelligence, the Gipe Nails were also uncommissioned. They went to the wee school wherein Mrs. O'Kane taught her brood with as much pride as Jean Brodie, and with perhaps as little success. With Confirmation fast approaching she knew her pupils would have to face a religious examination by the parish priest and she knew that the Nail who was in line to receive the sacrament would never pass it. So she had a word in Fr. Larkin's ear.

"Listen to this," she invited him one day when he dropped in to the schoolroom.

She called the boy over and said, "Stand there, please." He managed this.

"Now, say Ah!"

"Say Ah!" he responded obediently.

"No, you say Ah!" she explained.

"You say Ah!" he volunteered.

"I mean for you to say Ah!" she clarified.

"I mean for you to say Ah!" sang out the young Einstein.

"I see what you mean," agreed Fr. Larkin. "Don't worry, I'll ask something really easy just to save his face and it will be fine."

Came the day and, true to his word, when Fr. Larkin got to young Nail he pointed to a large picture of the Blessed Virgin which adorned a corner.

"Can you tell me who that is?" he asked.

After a pause the child answered dismissively,

"Ach, that's Eve or some of them fellas."

The father of this brood had married a girl from outside the townland who considered herself rather better than her neighbours, *tuppence ha'penny lookin' down on tuppence* they said. She attempted to make amends for the inbred lack of functioning cells by indoctrination, and managed to make them respond to some simple questions.

"What's your mother?"

"A lady."

"What's your father?"

"An oul' gipe."

But some lessons proved beyond them. She used to call them for their evening meal from the door of the house,

"Come in for your roast beef and cabbage" and no one was any the wiser until one evening when she had called them as usual, but stopped to speak to a passer-by. Before she could get back in to serve them a cry went up from within:

"Will we take them cowl or will we warm them?"

Porridge was always referred to in the plural.

The McStravicks had their own way with the culinary art. Cousin Dan O'Connell called with them one day when the father was preparing dinner for himself, cooking up a hearty fry on a cast-iron griddle on the range.

"Will you take a bite, son?" McStravick invited.

Dan declined, remembering that this was the family who killed their own pig in an upstairs bedroom and left it there to cure, with the blood making interesting patterns on the kitchen walls. A neighbour who was critical of the manner in which the pig was killed, if not the location, for it is indeed a skill which few then possessed and probably none now, commented,

"McStravick's no good when it comes to the pigs; he doesn't kill them, he only makes them die."

When the repast was ready, McStravick hauled himself closer to the range, threw his right leg over his left, lifted the griddle from the hob, set it on his knee and set to with a will, peering at Dan under the handle of the griddle as he talked.

They were always ready with their hospitality. My grandfather was visiting the house many years ago and was caught by an almighty thunderstorm.

"You needn't go home in that, Wilfred."

So the chat went on and the hour grew late and Wilfred waited to be shown a place to sleep. Eventually McStravick settled himself in his chair, turned up his coat collar and wished Wilfred goodnight, saying, as he closed his eyes,

"There's nowhere a man's as comfortable as in his own bed."

The women had retired to the lower room, the door of which now opened, and Mrs. McStravick hurled a nightshirt of indeterminate age and provenance towards her guest.

"Wrap that round ye, son," she advised.

My grandfather's closest friend in his youth was his first cousin, Tommy Duffin, and they use to write each other letters in verse. Only one of these has survived but in it, Tommy recalls a journey home after a ceilidh in Ballymulderg and he mentions a few of the families who made up the coterie.[1]

---

1 Appendix 1 includes a couple of the ditties we penned over the years, in case, like me, you have a taste for doggerel verse and oul' come-all-ye's.

Reader's Digest sometimes has a section entitled *Towards more colourful language*. Perhaps they should run a feature on Ballymulderg. One of the McStravicks walked with a slight limp; he was described as 'coming along on his oval wheel'. A mean man was a 'nabble'; 'Atty thra' was the name given to anyone who was crooked or 'thrawn'; someone thin was 'a wriggle o' bones'; James Johnston, telling us how he was swindled big-time by someone who had since gone bankrupt, explained: "I would have sued him, but you can't take britches off a bare ass" and a person whom you wanted to get rid of quickly was given a 'speedy gophant'.

Curiously I recently read Bernard MacLaverty's version in his novel *Grace Notes* – 'a speedy courante'; he muses on how the name of a French dance could have passed thus into Northern Irish speech, but I could have told him that to the residents of Ballymulderg that was nothing to get excited about; wasn't a heavy shower described as a 'quare plout'? Come along now, junior French speakers – It's raining: *Il pleut.*

The localisms would merit a book on their own, but I can't resist sneaking in one of my favourites. If something was in a precarious position, say near the edge of a table and likely to fall, my mother would admonish you,

"Watch that now, or it'll go its rakes brown ivy."

If she was in a hurry she would say,

"It'll go its rakes."

I have never been able to work out the origins of that one; but colourful language? Glorious Technicolor.

Lies, Damned Lies and Storytellers

"Me and O'Connell here," said Tommy Joe, "were playing cards one night down at the aerodrome in Ardboe, the time the Yanks were there."

"During the War?"

"Aye. Anyway, we were playing away and O'Connell was winnin', when suddenly this big sergeant comes in lookin' at his watch. 'Time to go, boys,' says he.

"We thought it was a ruse and sez I 'Where are ye going?' and this other big fella says,

'We're due a raid over Berlin; d'ye want to come?'

"Now O'Connell had never been in a plane before either, so we said all right, and aff we went. O'course we had to get all dressed up in the gear, you know, goggles, gloves, leather jackets, the works. The boys were terrible daycent and loaned us all we needed. It wasn't long before Berlin came in sight, and be Jaysus them boys dropped bomb after bomb on it like nobody's business."

"Were you scared?"

"Ach not really, till the big guns started; they were trying to get us outa the sky, you see; it was a bit noisy. But the crew we were with were smart enough, and sure it wasn't long before we had turned for home. Back we comes to Ardboe and finished the game of cards."

All this, in response to a simple question,

"Were you ever in a plane, Tommy Joe?"

He was a master of invention who could turn any comment, however unpromising, into a multi-faceted tale of great detail, without preamble or preparation. 'O'Connell' was my mother's cousin, Dan, a friend and neighbour of Tommy Joe, and he often found himself named as an accomplice in the latter's tales as a means of lending credence to the narrative, a circumstance which bothered him not at all, since it fooled no one.

"You have your teeth out, Tommy Joe; did you never try dentures?"

"Sure my heart's broke with dentures. I've been to dentists the length and breadth of Northern Ireland, paid a fortune and more, and not a denture could be made to fit my mouth."

"Why's that?"

"Ach, bad dentists; they're not what they used to be. Me and O'Connell were out wan day looking at a motor over near Toome, and on the way back we called in for a bite at a wee hotel. There was a wedding going on, and even though we didn't know them, the bride came over and asked us in to the meal. You nivver saw such a spread as was set before us, but divil a bit of it could I ate without the teeth.

"Now, the woman who owned the hotel came round to see was everything all right, and when she came to me she says 'Is there something wrong with the food?' all concerned.

"'Divil a hate, missus,' says I; 'But I haven't a bar in me grate to enjoy it.'

"'Never mind,' she says, and off she goes and was back a minute later with a set of false teeth.

"'Try them,' says she.

"Well, I put the teeth in, and begod, you would think they were made for me. I ate me way through beef, and chicken, and vegetables, and apple tart, and biscuits and cake, and would'a' been ating yit if the food had kept coming.

"Back she comes at the end of the meal.

"'Well?' she says.

"'Missus,' says I, 'I'll give you any money for them teeth. Name your price.'

"'I'm terrible sorry,' she shook her head. 'They're not for sale.'

"'Not for sale!' I roared at her. 'If you knew the bother I have had trying to get teeth to fit me, you'd be giving them to me.'

"'Indeed,' she said, 'I would love to help; but those

teeth belonged to my late husband, and they have sentimental value.'"

As the old Irish saying goes, it's a poor thing that doesn't outlast a man.

Teeth have been known to cause quite a few problems, notably in getting a good fit and becoming used to wearing them. A farmer friend of ours was forced by the demise of his own choppers to be fitted with a set of delph, but would not admit as much to any of his acquaintances. One day he was at the local pig market and, in making what he hoped would be the clinching bid, got somewhat carried away, or rather his teeth did, and they flew into the ring where the animals were being paraded. Quick as a flash, he grabbed them and stuffed them back in his mouth before anyone would notice. Several days later he turned to a friend of ours and said,

"John, did you ever taste pig shit?"

"No," said John, "Never."

Your man turned and spat ruminatively at a target only he could see.

"You didn't miss much," he said.

Later on, his vanity overcome by discomfort, he only wore the teeth for state occasions. The rest of the time, they resided in the ashtray in the car, and were not infrequently thrown out with the contents.

One woman who cared nothing for appearance was the pig-woman, known throughout the North as a dealer who could more than hold her own in what was essentially a man's world. One day she was in full throttle in

————— ⬦ —————

Dungannon's Ann Street mart, revealing her toothless gums, when a rival dealer tried to get one over on her.

"Where do you buy your toothpaste?" he shouted loudly during a lull in the dealing.

"The same place you get your hair cream, you baldy-headed bastard," she retorted.

But aside from teeth, Tommy Joe had few rivals. He had a talent for mimicry that was unmatched by anyone I have ever known. Many's the evening Dan O'Connell would overhear a conversation taking place outside his window and identify two or three voices from the neighbourhood, only to emerge to find Tommy Joe in sole splendour, doubled up with laughter at having caught him out again. He had a knack for identifying idiosyncratic habits or turns of phrase, a certain way of clearing your throat, a stammer; and he had nicknames for everyone. He told us one day he had been to a demonstration of a new milking machine, and proceeded to describe its workings in detail. It was a minute or two before anyone realised the machine's noises were made up of a mixture of everyone's personal oddities: James Johnston's cough was the starter turning over; Bob Waterson's pet phrase was the engine running in – "'At right, 'at right, 'at right." Annie's nickname gave it full rein – "Mice eyes, mice eyes, mice eyes, mice eyes," Bob Steel gave it a change of gear with his habit of prefixing every utterance with "Eee..ah" and so it went on, and no one took offence, for wasn't everyone represented?

He did have one close runner-up in Lying Dan McKay, who recounted the grisly tale of how one day he set off for Derry to do some business before going out to mow in the Creagh meadows. Being tired after the journey, he decided to take a rest and, seeing no convenient park bench, he went up onto the walls and crept into Roaring Meg for a nap.

"Dammit," says he, "Didn't I forget they fire her off at noon, and I fell into a deep sleep, and the next thing I knew they were lighting the fuse at me arse, and away I went like a cannonball. But it worked out all right, for I landed right in the middle of the Creagh meadows where I wanted to be, and I picked myself up and started to mow. I was doing well, getting into my stride, when suddenly the scythe hit something solid. Wasn't there a tramp asleep in the long grass, and I had mowed the head clean off him! But I thought fast, and I picked it up and stuck it back on his neck, and he got up and lifted a second scythe, and mowed all day with me. I took him back to the house for a bite of supper, and we had great crack until he took a fit of coughing. He took out a handkerchief, blew his nose, and threw his head into the fire."

Lying Dan was a doggie man too.

"The best dog I ever had," he told us, "was a wee greyhound. He was as fast and smart and there nivvir was a hare yet that could bate him. When he died, I kind of missed him, so I had his hide tanned and made into a waistcoat, and d'ye know, you couldn't wear it out.

"I was out in the fields one day making hay, and it got terrible warm. I took off the waistcoat and left it in the ditch, and the next thing was, I started a big hare from the hay, and it took aff over the field, and the waist-coat after it, and I never saw hilt nor hide of either one again.

"And I wouldn't have minded," he added after a pause, "If it hadn't been for the gold watch I had in the waist-coat pocket."

Mind you, the Liar McKerney from Tyrone was no goat's toe when it came to stories.

"I was in America one time, riding the trains," he said, "And the trains there are far longer than ours, seventy or eighty carriages no bother, and that's the small ones. I was dying for a smoke, but I had neither matches nor lighter and damn the one in the carriage with me smoked. I was gasping.

"This boyo sitting opposite me says, 'You'll be all right at the next bend'.

"I didn't know what he was on about, but I soon found out. We faced this bend in the track and I swear to God, you never saw a hairpin bend till you saw this. Sharp wouldn't be in it. The train turned back on herself till I thought we would be run over, and all the regulars just leaned over to the one side till she was round. Then she straightened out and away we went."

Did he get his smoke?

"Oh aye, I leaned out and got a light off the engine driver."

But I have to award the last word to Tommy Joe, for I never met his equal for invention. He and Dan were in a pub one night having a yarn, and a young whipper-snapper at the bar tried to get a rise out of this old fellow, showing off his own street-smart humour. After ignoring him for a while, Tommy Joe turned to Dan and announced,

"Do you see thon yahoo at the end of the bar? He's threatened with intelligence."

"Do you think so?" queried Dan.

"I know so. And most of them haven't the real thing at all, only a kind of peasant cunning."

I reckon he was right.

Siblings and Others

My mother had three siblings: an elder brother, Charlie who, when his father emigrated to the USA, took on willy-nilly the role of father figure, and was hero-worshipped by the other three as a result; a younger sister, Mona; and the baby of them all, brother Wilfred. They were all born at home in the fashion of the day, delivered by the family doctor, often with the help of a midwife or local woman, sometimes not. Dr Patrick Kirlan was childless, and at Mona's birth he requested that she be named after him, for he loved children. But a promise had already been given to name her after her aunt Monica, her father's sister, so she became Monica Patricia, later Monica Pat and later still, just Mona.

She was small and fair, as delicate as an angel, with enormous eyes that throughout her life would elicit

extravagant compliments from anyone who met her. Her
hair darkened to a mid-brown as she grew and retained
its baby softness, from which, as a young woman in the
era of Marcel waves and peek-a-boo bangs, she derived
no little heartache. Her skin was the best I have ever
seen, surviving attack by all kinds of cleaning agents,
including carbolic soap, for above all, Mona liked to
be clean. Bella Mallon, a gentle elderly neighbour of
ours, always maintained that Mona resembled no one
as much as The Blessed Virgin, with such sincerity that
one could only agree. We decided that she must have
been referring to a particular likeness of this august per-
sonage, but we were never quite sure, although at that
stage of her existence, she was unlikely to have met the
real thing. Throughout her life Mona's style was girl-
ish where my mother's was severe – Mona was Laura
Ashley; Maureen was Chanel.

There was a tomboy streak in Mona that belied her
fragile femininity. She desperately wanted to be a boy
and, at four years of age decided that the way to bring
about the desired transformation was to tuck her dress
into her knickers and her thumbs into the waistband
elastic, and go about whistling as boys did. The consternation this must have caused in 1927 can only be
imagined.

Her idol as a child was a neighbour man, Jim Sampson
(Dim), who provided her with a ready ally and, inadvertently, her first (and only!) swearword – another
prerequisite for being a boy. Coming into the kitchen
one day, Jim fell over the family cat who shot out from

———— ∞ ————

under the range and made for the door as he entered. He hurled the nearest available missile at the rapidly departing creature and shouted after it,

"Go to hell, ye oul' bitch ye!"

Ever after, when annoyed or cross, Mona could be heard to mutter,

"Goa hell oul' bish."

She adored her father, and it broke her small heart when he emigrated to the USA. Whenever she was scolded, upset, or accused of any misdemeanour, she would threaten to go to 'Amackery' to be with him. One day she set out to do just that – walking, and equipped with just the clothes she stood up in, and the child's conviction that the simple act of going would actually get her there. Halfway down the long loanin that led to the main road she began to regret her impulsiveness, but pride kept her going, despite tired feet and growing misgivings. But salvation was at hand in the form of Dim, who happened to be heading for a visit to the house.

"Where are ye going, daughter?"

"I'm going to Amackery," she told him doggedly, appending her tale of woe.

"You're just right," said Jim, the master of psychology, "But if I were you, I'd go back to the house and get me coat."

Salvation comes in many guises.

She grew into a beautiful woman who, despite seventeen marriage proposals, never married, a circumstance for which I had cause to be grateful, for she lived with us most of her life and was to me friend, sister, aunt, mentor and confidante, never failing in her love for me, always supportive, yet constructively critical, and demanding of a high standard of social grace and behaviour. Even yet, sixteen years after a brain haemorrhage took her from us, her influence still informs my conduct. I often think, *What would Mona say?* and can imagine her quiet voice telling me in no uncertain terms exactly where she stood on any number of issues. She was wise beyond reason, funny and learned; never censorious, but honest and direct. She never offended anyone, but always made her point, and if she was your friend, would defend you to the death. I recall a jealous associate of ours saying, when I was accepted to read English at Trinity,

"Why is Aideen, with *her* brains, going to *Trinity?*"

To which Mona quietly replied,

"Well, it was good enough for most of Ireland's writers, poets and statesmen from the seventeenth century on, so it'll hardly do her any harm."

She was a perfect foil for my mother who enjoyed being centre-stage; she was the born storyteller, Mona the back up. "Tell them about the time..." she'd say, and Maureen would accept the cue with the precision of a professional orator. During a particularly lengthy recital, Mona and I would make the tea.

Among her many admirers were several whom she favoured. There was John Vray, a tall Texan with a lazy southern drawl who called her 'Honey' and wanted to take her back to his ranch, but she could never separate him from the Hollywood image of the cowboy, and never quite took him seriously. Then there was René, a Belgian medic who was with the medical corps stationed in Dungannon during the War. Because his English was imperfect, he often misunderstood what was being said to him, and she could not altogether rid herself of the impression that he was half-witted. This was exacerbated by a letter that came one day asking her to sue him for breach of promise! The story was that he had had a girlfriend in Namur in Belgium before he had met Mona, and though no formal engagement existed between them, the girl and her family assumed there was an understanding, even though René's family did not approve of her because she was 'of the people'! To avoid having to do an ungentlemanly thing and tell her he did not care for her, René hit upon the breach of promise idea, hoping it would bring everything to the desired conclusion; but Mona was aghast. No amount of persuasion would move her, not even the list of referees who would attest to his good name, and René became history. Perhaps it was just as well. The story is told of two brothers from The Moy who were discovered one day rowing their sister through flooded meadows in a tin bath. The reason? She was to marry a Belgian, and they were trying to accustom her to the long sea journey ahead of her.

Naturally I never met René, but his letters to Mona reveal a young man of principle who, though a bit wet behind the ears, is very likeable. He writes to her from France in 1945,

———— ∞ ————

'... I am a little sad because I am an idealist young man and I know that perfection cannot be reached in this world ... Do you understand why I don't like life in Army?[1] I like moral perfection, chiefly on conduct about girls ... I am sad to see married men to run for girls here, when their women are waiting in Belgium. Englishmen and Yankees are doing the same thing in Belgium and in France, but I am Catholic (by religion) and I think that to do wrong for wrong is not correct. The life in this world is sad ...'

One of his most endearing letters (for me) is this one from Belgium:

'You know that at Portadown some men are going often in the street with drums (10 or 15 men). They beat the drum with fury. In the country there are also men with drums. What is the signification?'

And he says,

'The military service is not yet finished, and I cannot say when it will finish, I hope for May, a pretty month for marriage ... I regret Ireland and his hills.'

The love of her life was Sgt. Ernest Price, who hailed from West Virginia. They met in Dungannon, and kept

---

1. Like many Belgians stationed here at the end of the War, René was a conscript.

in touch for a long time, throughout which she could never screw her courage to the sticking point and make the journey to America – despite her youthful ambitions! This was no wartime romance, forged in a crucible of unreality to fizzle out when saner times returned; their relationship lasted for upwards of ten years. Ernest was sincere, generous, serious, a lover of books and music. Wherever he went with his regiment, he spent time getting to know the area, its history and its culture. He writes to Mona about the Black Forest, the places he has visited that are mentioned in folklore, the damage inflicted on Munich by the war. His letters are full of snippets for the social historian – in 1948, it took four days for a letter to get from Dungannon to West Virginia; Jameson whiskey cost seventy shillings a bottle (that's three pounds fifty for you young'uns); even in the States, you had to queue for 'hose'. And he asks her,

'Did you know they were made from coal, air and water? They manufacture dresses here from milk and from spun glass. Would you like one?'

There was a period of about eighteen months when she did not hear from him then, out of the blue, a letter. He had been wounded, and there were fears he would not walk again; rather than burden her with that, he ceased communication until the prognosis was better and he was on the mend. But the fates were against them; Mona deliberated; Ernest's career did not prosper as he had hoped and around 1948, he re-enlisted in the army and resumed his medical training. The last letter we have tells of his requesting a European posting. He was killed in Korea.

Right up to the '70s, Mona was fending off prospective suitors, but I truly believe that after Ernest, no one ever seriously engaged her affections again.

Mona's repertoire of songs, ballads and come-all-ye's was extensive, and she used it to great effect while baby-sitting. And later! I recall a particularly wet and miserable day we spent in Fermanagh, a most lovely part of Ireland when it's dry; but it rarely is. We stuck it out for a long time, but finally admitted defeat. Four wet, bedraggled humans and one disgruntled dog headed home to Dungannon, disappointed and with tempers fraying. Somewhere above Ballygawley, Mona launched into the following ditty, sung to the tune of *Dolly Grey*.

See his teeth they are like pearls,
And his dandy little curls,
And his name is Harry Mortimer Devere;
It's the pleasure of my life
Very soon to be his wife
And these words I will no longer have to hear:

Goodbye darling I must leave you,
Though it breaks my heart to go;
I'll be back tomorrow night,
If I do not come I'll write,
Just a word or two to let my darling know.

This was followed by *The Scavenger's Cart, The Factory Girl* and many more humorous or maudlin offerings that had us laughing all the way home.

She detested pretension, having time only for 'real people'; and had a keen eye (and ear!) for the ridiculous; and she had an abiding fear of ghosts. My mother and Wilf ruthlessly exploited this weakness. The house they lived in as children was a three-storey Edwardian terrace house, with a toilet in the basement. When going through a phase of using this facility late at night, Mona insisted the other two come with her, Wilf in front, herself in the middle, holding a candle or small oil lamp, and mum bringing up the rear. This arrangement was designed to ensure that if something was waiting at the foot of the stairs, it would grab Wilf; anything following them down from behind would get my mother, while Mona made a clean getaway. This did not appeal to the other two, and it ended abruptly one night when Wilf descended quicker than had been agreed and as Mona reached the last step, he turned back and blew out the candle. He melted into the darkness while Maureen fled back upstairs, leaving Mona benighted and hysterical. Of course my grandmother chastised the two miscreants roundly, but the ruse worked. Mona ceased her midnight ramblings.

She had a phenomenal memory, a characteristic shared by all four of them, especially when it came to poetry. She and my mother could act out the courtroom scene from *The Merchant of Venice* word perfectly; she asked me one day if I recognised a scene from Shakespeare that began,

'Must thou with hot irons burn out both mine eyes?'
'Young boy, I must.'

She then proceeded to quote a whole scene from one of the history plays, *Henry V*, I think, that she had studied fifty years before in school.

"I thought of it last night in bed," she said.

A frequent visitor to our house who occupies a chapter of his own later on[2] used to say that he enjoyed nothing better than a good argument with Maureen and Mona, but he couldn't compete when they started quoting poetry to support their point of view.

An amazing memory is about the only thing she shared with brother Wilf; they really were as different as chalk and cheese. He was a roustabout, she was a lady; he was through-other, she was pins on paper. He recalled being followed around while he was doing any of the DIY jobs of which he was a master by a dustpan-wielding Mona, who was lifting dust even before it hit the floor. Not unnaturally, this drove him crazy. Wilf had a red-hot temper, and once, when he had spent an entire day putting a window into the jamb wall to admit more light into the kitchen, he warned her not to clean the glass until the putty had time to set. Getting his back turned for a second, Mona thought she would give it a wee wipe, just to get the finger marks off. Everyone heard the crack. Seconds later, there was blood everywhere – his, not hers, for he had put his fist right through the glass. In the days before a phone in every

2. See chapter 10 'Dr Who'

house and a car at every door, half the neighbours were drafted in to get him to hospital.

Indeed he was no stranger to hospitals; they were almost his second home. He led a charmed life after an inauspicious start and, though a walking disaster area from his early days, he fought off all challenges until the final one from cancer caught him with his defences down, or at a time when he was just tired of fighting.

He chose to come into the world after six months' gestation instead of the more usual nine, on a night when my grandmother was in the throes of a violent migraine attack. He was born breech, with a broken foot and a black eye after a forceps delivery, and without nails, eyebrows, or anything else that might have made him look less like a skinned rabbit. Dr Kirlan's instructions to the nurse were to put the baby, which he held out to her on the palm of his hand, somewhere to die, and come back and help him attend to the mother who was very ill. And so it was that Wilfred John Joseph Campbell was handed to his grandmother, Britta, in a shoe box, to be set inside the hearth fender, and watched over until he died, for this was a country farmhouse in 1925, with no nearby neo-natal baby unit built to deal with such emergencies. But Britta recognised the spark of life in the baby's eyes, a sign of the fighting spirit that saved his life on many a subsequent occasion, and she began to feed him from a dropper, with milk laced with a little whiskey, a practice to which he later attributed his fondness for *uisce beatha* as well as his survival. He began to thrive, with such success that when he was taken, at age three, to the American Embassy to apply for emigration papers, the doctor who examined him nicknamed him 'The Burster.'

Some time later it appears that Mona observed the baby's nappy being changed and immediately declared him a 'dirty wee bish'. Nurse Maguire, who held to the view that all children should be like the birds who in their little nests agree, tried to persuade her otherwise, but Mona would have none of it. She would not even enter the room where he was. One day the good nurse, weary of rhetoric, resorted to that other time-honoured means of persuasion – bribery. Mona should have a chocolate bar if she would kiss the new arrival. Hygiene struggled with desire but the chocolate tipped the scale. She was led to the cot where she subjected the baby to intense scrutiny before tentatively kissing him – on his little finger. She seized the chocolate and ran, to be discovered moments later at the kitchen sink scrubbing her mouth and muttering, "Dirty wee bish."

But throughout his life he was dogged by health problems and mishaps. At about two years old he developed tonsillitis and an operation was deemed necessary. A surgeon was brought from the Mid-Ulster hospital to perform the surgery at home, but Wilf turned out to be immune to chloroform, and despite all they could do he could not be anaesthetised, so he was operated upon wide awake with his tongue gagged to the side of his mouth. For years afterwards he suffered nightmares, hallucinations and claustrophobia, and the sight of anyone wearing white sent him into hysterics. But again he overcame this, and when, at seven or eight years old, he was savaged by a greyhound bitch who thought he was attacking her pups, he took it in his stride.

In his thirties he developed a mastoid behind his ear and needed a major operation to remove it, in which, according to the surgeon, the margin for error that could result in brain damage was as thin as a cigarette paper. He was left profoundly deaf in one ear, but as sharp as ever in the brains department.

He survived a fall from scaffolding of about 120 feet, a tumble from a ladder that shattered his heel, and a motor accident in which he was thrown through the windscreen of a car, over an underpass to the motorway forty feet below. Eighteen months of residency in Birmingham's accident hospital followed, during which time he was encased in tinfoil for days on end to prevent pneumonia, and once more he came through.

He was incredibly clever with his hands; according to my mother, he could put a leg to a cat, and in Dungannon in the '50s there was hardly a house he hadn't been called to, to 'do a wee job'. Had he charged anyone for these jobs he could have been a millionaire; Bill Gates would only have been in the ha'penny place. He was immensely innovative in his approach to materials and technique. When he was wiring a room for Mrs. Forbes he ran out of wire. Since most people in Dungannon, or at least those of my acquaintance, were semi-nocturnal, this was probably the middle of the night and there was nowhere open to buy more, so Wilf stripped out the clothesline, the old-fashioned kind that was made from twisted wire, and used that. When Mrs. Forbes finally sold the house in the '80s she told us that Wilf's wiring was intact, and had never given her any bother.

He was putting a window into a snug for a pub-owning friend in Birmingham, and he went to a salvage yard for the glass.

"How big do you want it, mate?" enquired the man.

"About that by that," said Wilf, forming his hands into a semblance of a rectangle.

"About that by that," mimicked the man. "Are you mad?"

"No," said Wilf. "If you'll sort it out for me, I'll nip over to the pub for a pint and be back in a minute."

Several minutes and pints later he returned to find a likely looking pane of glass awaiting him.

"There you are," said the man, "but it'll never fit. What kind of a measurement is 'that by that'?"

"It'll fit," said Wilf, paying him, "for I haven't made the window yet."

As a child I adored Wilf. He was one of those rare people who actually do like children, not in a sentimental sort of way but as beings in their own right. He never talked down to children, but gave them their own time, a gift he shared with Charlie, who had time for everybody. I would be waiting for Wilf to come home from work and I always got a ride on his shoulders or on the bar of his bike. He would invite me to 'pick a pocket', and I would select right or left in trousers or jacket; the contents were mine. He never cheated; if the pocket was empty (which was rare) I went without; but if it contained a half-crown (a vast sum in those days) it was handed over. One night he gave me so much money that I was in O'Neill's shop buying for all my pals, and Mrs. O'Neill sent for my mother.

"It's not that I mind, Maureen," she explained. "It's just that I don't want you to think I'm taking that child's money box off her."

"Never worry, Phil," said Mum, "She got it from Wilf."

"Och, if I'd known that …"

I was always a picky eater, so Wilf would set me on his knee and divide his dinner in two.

"Let's see who'll be finished first."

This always worked better than Mum's pleas to take just one more bite.

I imbibed the family's love of poetry at an early age. Indeed it could not have been otherwise, for as often as not my bedtime story was in verse, and a particular favourite was Tennyson's *The May Queen*. I did not know anything about Victorian sentimentality, but the tale of the little girl who dies the spring after her triumph as Queen of the May always reduced me to tears, a fact wholly overlooked by my mother and Mona who were concentrating on reading it to me until one night, enter Wilf. Shortly after the reading began he began to mutter.

"Jaysus, that's tarra…that's not right…I'll have to send for the Cruelty…ach, have yiz no sense…"

Eventually tiring of these interruptions, Mona said,

———— ∞ ————

"What is wrong with you, Wilf?"

Whereupon he mimed the wiping of tears from his own cheek and pointed to me, and only then did they notice I was in floods. But I adored the thing, and insisted upon its recital nightly.

Wilf had a memory that retained songs and verses gathered from a forty-year acquaintance with *Ireland's Own*, as well as most of Robert Service's Yukon output, and a host of ditties from God knows where. He loved to recite, and he did so with pipe in hand and his eye firmly fixed on one person in the audience, while we were transfixed by his delivery. He sang most songs in the same key, and many of them to the same air, but the humour of *Me Oul' Skelara Hat*, *The Bright Silvery Light of the Moon*, or *The Oul' Clothes Shop* made you overlook such detail; and we joined with gusto in the choruses:

Oh, we sell corduroy, some of the best of tweed,
Waistcoats, petticoats, they're all of the walking breed;
We never purchase an article unless it's ready to hop,
And we're doing a roaring business outa the Oul
Clothes Shop.

His choice of lullaby was often unconventional; it's not the first time I've fallen asleep to the strains of *Johnson's Motor Car!*

Charlie, the eldest, was frequently likened to Gary Cooper, and indeed had the same kind of gentle, manly, laconic personality that 'Coop' presented in many of his screen roles; not surprisingly, he was one of Charlie's movie idols in an era when everyone went to the pictures, and everyone had a favourite star. He too was a skilled raconteur, but would never have been prevailed upon to sing, and he held his audience more by dint of a genuine interest in every individual present than through dramatic artifice. He had two guiding principles in life – never take offence where none is intended, and very seldom where it is; and give everyone you meet a boost; and these, together with his deep religious faith which he regarded as 'a sheet anchor', defined his attitude to the world around him.

He was the greatest lover of reading I have ever known; when he opened a book, he effectively lost touch with reality. Many's the day his wife, Anne, would come home to a house in turmoil. Having left him to baby-sit their two young daughters, she would find him immersed in a volume of poetry picked up in the Bullring in Birmingham where they lived at the time, and the children running riot about the place. The last straw was when she found them playing with their Santa Claus gifts, two beautiful dolls, one night in November.

"Jesus, Mary and Joseph, Charlie! Where did they get those?"

"Ach, sure I found them on top of the wardrobe and thought they would like them."

He was tall and inclined to stoop a little, but he always squared his shoulders as he went out the front door, as if preparing to meet a challenge; and he had a forelock that defied the assistance of Brylcreem to keep it in place. He had a ready explanation for this.

"John Johnston put that in with a curling tongs twenty years ago."

Oddly enough, no matter how old he got, it was always twenty years ago. I would give much to get my hands on a pair of tongs such as John used, for so effective were they, that not only did their work last Charlie his lifetime, but they actually made the quiff hereditary; my own hair has the very same tendency to this day!

Charlie never criticised anyone; he would listen awhile as the rest of the family vented their spleen and then say quietly,

"Sure you never know what problems that crayther might have at home."

It always made us stop and think.

He treated everyone with respect and quiet courtesy, and had the knack of making you feel that you were the most important person in the world when he talked to you. Despite moving to Dungannon his heart remained in Ballymulderg, but like his father before him, lack of money and the untenable situation between my grandmother and his Uncle Tom forced him to leave, and he went to Birmingham, which he detested, describing it as 'Pomeroy enlarged'. He never intended to stay, but England in the '50s was the graveyard of many Irish hopes and many Irish people; and his early death at fifty-one pre-empted his dreams of coming home. During one sojourn back to Dungannon, he met an old resident who greeted him with,

———— ∞ ————

"Ach, Charlie Campbell – Dungannon's greatest loss."

It's an epitaph he would have been honoured by, when his early death at only fifty-one from Hodgkin's Disease robbed the family of its elder statesman, and all of us of a good friend.

Every acquaintance became a friend, but he particularly sought the company of older men, rightly enjoying their wisdom and humour. One of his favourites was Paddy Doran, sire of a family whom we are pleased to number amongst our best friends. Paddy was a plumber to trade and had a bicycle shop, but he could turn his hand to anything if he chose to. He was summoned to a local hotel one night to open the safe which unaccountably had jammed. After working away for some time, Paddy released it.

"How much will that be, Mr Doran?" enquired Madame, wife of the proprietor. Now, Paddy never charged anyone enough for any job, so when he asked for ten bob, it was probably worth about three times that. But Madame was famed for her parsimoniousness, and was duly appalled.

"Mr Doran, that's monstrous! I couldn't possibly pay that."

"That's all right," said Paddy gathering up his tools and preparing to leave; then he slammed the safe door shut. "Good night, then."

"Mr Doran, you'll have to open that door again, you told me the lock was faulty."

"It is, and I will," replied Paddy. "But it'll cost you fifteen bob if I do."

Madame paid up.

On another occasion, Charlie had called for Paddy to go to the pictures. As they prepared to leave the house Paddy said to his wife,

"If that oul' bitch calls for her bike, Eileen, it's ready. Tell her it'll be half a crown."

They got to the door and Paddy said,

"Hold on, son, it's coul out, I'll need a cap," and he went back in.

"Eileen, if that oul' bitch calls for her bike, tell her it's five bob. Are you right, Charlie?"

"Aye, Paddy."

"D'ye know, it's a bitter night; a body would need a scarf. Hold on a minute."

Action replay, then:

"Eileen, if that oul' bitch calls for her bike, tell her it'll be seven-and-six. Come on now, we'll be late."

Again the door was reached.

"I never felt as sharp a wind; I'm damned but I'll need gloves. Eileen, if that oul' bitch calls for her bike, charge her ten bob. Come on, Charlie, what's keeping ye?"

Wilf went to Paddy one day and asked him to come and look at what he thought was a burst pipe in the street outside the house.

"Sure a minute'll fix that son; you don't need me; here, take any tools you need."

Wilf was delighted to be entrusted thus, until a wet and cramped hour later he realised how neatly he'd been had. The job was fiddly, messy and very sore on the back. Experience tells.

And so the same gene pool produced these four very different and yet oddly similar characters: Charlie, gentle and unassuming yet with a formidable intellect; Wilf, nicknamed 'The Quare Fella' and known to his pals as 'The Wolf', quick to anger, slow to condemn, a master of many trades and dabbler in all; Mona, called 'Lady Mona' because of her refinement and by one admirer, 'Monavanna', after, I believe, an old song; described by a very good friend as 'The nicest girl that ever walked the streets of Dungannon,' with no idea of the classic double entendre he was guilty of; and my mother, Carmen Miranda with her turban and cigarette holder, her stories and her spirit. The two sisters were so different in nature that it was often commented upon by friends. Teesie Ritchie, our next door neighbour, remarked,

"Mona's a nice girl, but Maureen's a sharper"; and on a later occasion,

"Mona was a nicer girl until she started running about with Maureen," no doubt after she had felt the sharp edge of one or other's tongue.

But the ultimate comparison has to belong to Christie McFaul, a delightful character, who always stood me a bottle of Lucozade when he met me in Kathleen O'Neill's shop with the remark,

"You'll make it, girl."

"I'm very fond of them two Campbell girls," he said. "Mona's a lady, and Maureen's a rummelly thump."

No. I don't know either!

What Everybody Needs

When my mother's family first came to Dungannon, they lived in Irish Street for a while before moving to the Donaghmore Road, where I grew up. It was always identifiable as a wee community in itself, for although it became Ann Street just by turning a corner, and transmuted into the Lower Donaghmore Road by dint of passing the Sprickly Well, it was nonetheless regarded by its inhabitants and outsiders alike as a self-contained unit. It might have had connections with the wider world; indeed, it was always well aware of its doings, but it was serene in its own completeness.

This resulted partly from the fact that everybody knew everyone else, seed, breed and generation, and from the habit, common throughout Ireland in those bygone days, of leaving one's door open so that anyone might come in; if you waited long enough, someone always did. Most people there sprang from Dungannon stock, and so their forebears knew each other too. That my grandmother and her brood were so readily accepted into this close-knit community is testimony, I believe, to two factors: her own gentle nature and innate reserve, which meant that while ready to befriend anyone, she kept her own counsel and confided in no one; and the warmth and generosity of the Dungannon people, who recognised in her a proud woman forced to struggle against the odds, and who respected her stance and her need to remain both friendly and aloof. This generosity of spirit, I might add, I have never seen equalled anywhere else.

The row of houses wherein we dwelt was an Edwardian terrace of twelve: six and six, divided by 'the entry'. The houses were two storeys at the front and three at the back because of a cellar which, in my time, most people had converted into a kitchen. The houses were high, narrow, damp and cold, but I can safely say that I for one never had an unhappy day in that place. Looking back, it is clear that there were more similarities between my mother's childhood in the '20s and mine in the '50s, than between my childhood and that of my friends' children in the '80s and '90s. I played the same games as she did: *hopscotch, tig, hide-and-seek;* we made *cat'n'bats,* played *The Farmer Wants a Wife, March the Robbers, Dusty Bluebells* and *Down on the Carpet.* We skipped to *Vote, Vote, Vote* and played ball games like *Birella Birella* and a dozen more. Summer days were long and warm, and we were allowed to stay out until the streetlights came on at dusk and the bats came out.

We always called neighbour women 'Mrs.' First name terms were for adults only, and then only between long-standing acquaintances. Our house was number 6 at one time and then, when new houses were built further down, we unaccountably became 25. Mrs. Ritchie lived on one side, Mrs. Kelly on the other. Mrs. Ritchie (Teesie) was in her youth a dressmaker or, in the parlance of the day, a tailoress. She was known as 'the Paris model', such was her sense of style, and it was rumoured that her estimates of how much fabric you would need to make a garment tended to err on the generous, so that she and her offspring were always kitted out in the latest fashion. Her daughter Mandy was a few years older than me, and by all accounts was something of a tearaway. Stories abound of her having the whole street in a turmoil one day when she disappeared for hours without trace, only to crawl out of the oven just as the police were about to be summoned, saying, "Did you miss me?" Then there was the time her mother sent her to the door to fend off an irate customer whose order Teesie had failed to complete on time.

"Is your mother in, love?"

"No."

"Are you sure?"

"Aye."

"Did she leave a message for me?"

"No."

"Well, what time will she be back?" This one she had not been counselled for.

"Hold on and I'll go down and ask her."

Or again, answering the door, but this time with no fending off to do, she greeted a customer with,

"Who are you anyway?" to which her caller replied,

"I'm Brodisan; your mammy's expecting me."

Mandy beamed. "Well, I'm a Catholic, but come on in anyway."

Many stories exist of her swearing, a habit she had picked up at an early age and relished throughout her childhood, though in adulthood I never heard her say anything untoward. One day she had climbed a high wall at the top of Ann Street, a favourite pastime of local children, but Mandy, being small, got stuck. A retired teacher who was known for his surliness came upon her plight and stopped to assess the scene. Seeing that she was in real difficulty, he laid down his umbrella which he was never without, took his folded overcoat from his arm where it neatly reposed and laid it carefully on the ground, and prepared to lift her down from her perch. As he did so, he remonstrated with her on the folly of children getting into such scrapes in the first place; Mandy replied with a string of abuse which cast serious doubts on his parentage, so he released his grip on her waist, turned and picked up his coat and brolly, solemnly bade her good day and left her to shift for herself. Hearing of the incident later my mother said to her,

"It wasn't such a good idea to swear at him, Mandy."

"Ach no, Mrs. D'Arcy, I know, but I've given it up now," she said.

"That's good; and so you don't curse at all?"

"Ach well," said Mandy, shamed into truthfulness, "I might call the Dean an oul' b****** now and again, but that's all."

My mother never did find out what the poor man had done to deserve this; but she did find out why it was that Mandy was sent home from school in her first few weeks until she had learned manners. It happened that the school doctor came on a visit, and Mandy was totally unprepared for what was to come. A good friend of ours who had gone in to collect her own child caught sight of Mandy perched up on a desk shrieking with indignation as the nuns sought to pacify her, one speaking soothing words while another sprinkled her liberally with Holy Water (my uncle Wilf's assertion that a third stood by with a dictionary I take to be false). The woman hastened on but Mandy's voice echoed down the corridor,

"He's nothing but an oul' b******; he stuck a f****** needle in me arm, so he did."

Another neighbour and friend in need was Alice McGeary, described by my father as "the cleanest woman I ever saw." She was what my mother called 'sonsy' – not fat, but comfortable, salt of the earth and capable and full of crack. She had lovely light auburn hair, which she wore scraped off her face in a bun, and always sported one of those wraparound overalls that you never see today. She loved stories, especially ghost stories, and could tell a good one; and often prefixed her account with "Hell to yer sowl". I used to think this an odd phrase for a kindly and God-fearing woman, but I now believe it to have been a corruption of 'Health to your soul', which would sit more readily on her conscience; a blessing in disguise, you might say.

"Did you ever hear the Banshee, Alice?"

"Hel' to yer sowl, didn't I see her sittin' on our windy stool wringin' her hands and cryin' the night before oul' Jimmy Carberry died."

"They say he's been *seen*."

"Aye, I seen him a wheen of nights ago, down the back; milking the goat and singing Bonny Mary of Argyle, as large as life."

It was this good woman to whom my uncle slipped the potin on that never-to-be-forgotten Christmas Eve, when she had to be oxter-coggled home three or four yards from our house to hers.[2]

She was married twice, and it was her second husband, Francie, who was known to me. A big gentle giant, he was as rough as ropes, and I can well believe a story that was told of him as follows. Alice was in the early stages of a pregnancy and felt unwell in the night, so she wakened Francie and sent him for the doctor.

"Tell him I'm afraid of a miscarriage," she warned him.

As Dr Campbell got ready he said, "Do you know what's wrong, Francie; what way is she?"

"I don't know a damn, Doctor," roared Francie, "but she says it's something with wheels on it."

This may be apocryphal, but he did go up to Doran's one day to report a faulty tap in the kitchen. Not a man to waste words, he shouted from the shop doorway,

"Paddy, come up and take a look at Alice's water."

2. See chapter 7. 'The Spirit World'

He once took a friend of ours, Veronica Rice, to Belfast, I forget why, but he offered to buy her tea in a hotel. Now this was a rare treat in those days, and Veronica was young, but she told my mother that it was the evening from Hell. Francie marched her to a table right in the centre of the dining room, admonished her not to give a damn about 'themmuns looking at us', and delivered a running commentary on the meal, the hotel and their fellow diners.

When coffee was served in china coffee cups, he expostulated,

"Jaysus! Eggcups!" and then threw the beverage into the saucer to cool it.

Further up the street lived Maggie Heyburn. She wore a man's cap and men's shoes, kept lodgers and looked after her brother Hughie, a painter to trade and a martyr to drink. When he ran out of money and was on the tear he would appeal to Maggie. One day she refused him; he threatened suicide; she held firm. He retreated to his room in high dudgeon, and Maggie left him until it was time for tea. When she went to call him she found him stretched on the bed dripping gore, a cut-throat razor in his hand and a pool of red on the floor. Maggie ran for the neighbours, filled with remorse, and soon a posse had arrived, hotly debating who would enter the chamber of horror first. Only the presence of the assembled folk prevented the 'suicide' from becoming murder, when Hughie was discovered hale and hearty cleaning up the mess a tin of red paint had made.

Maggie had a collection of small china ornaments on

her sideboard, all firmly stuck down so that the lodgers couldn't steal them; one had a cap which came off, and this she would doff to visiting dignitaries. When old age pensions were introduced, an earnest young man came to interview her and assess her claim.

"Have you any relatives?" he enquired.

"A field full of them in Ardboe," she told him.

"Do you own any land?" he pursued.

"I do," says Maggie, going into the kitchen and emerging with two flowerpots. "That's it."

She had an incredibly infectious laugh which literally bent her double when she gave it full rein, and she called anything whose proper name escaped her a 'charley', as we might say a 'thingummy' today. She sent my aunt Mona, then a young girl, to the local shop for 'a long charley'; embarrassed, Mona told Mrs. O'Neill of her errand. Unfazed, Big Annie handed her one of those elliptical currant loaves with icing on the top; needless to say, in our house, we never called them anything else thereafter.

Mrs. Donnelly called to see Maggie one day when she was growing older, and found her airing a pile of clothing on a horse before the fire, among them the sensible interlock knickers to which Maggie had attached knee pads to keep the rheumatism at bay.

"You shouldn't do so much washing at once, Maggie," she advised, "it's too much for you."

"Ach, Annie daughter, sure that's only my change of clothes."

It was after this that Mrs. Donnelly tried to persuade

———— ∞ ————

Maggie to use the laundry, and offered to put a load in with her own on the next collection day. Far from being pleased upon its return, Maggie was incensed.

"Annie, they're nothing but a pack of rogues," she raged. "They cut the charleys off my knickers."

"I wouldn't have minded," Mrs. Donnelly later told my mother, "but they must have thought they were mine!"

Big Annie, or Mrs. O'Neill to the youngsters, owned the local shop, which later passed to her daughter Kathleen, one of my mother's oldest and dearest friends. It was the place where everyone congregated for a chat; the exchange and mart for all the women of the neighbourhood. No wonder Maureen called it GHQ. When my mother disappeared for any length of time, my dad would send me up to O'Neill's to find her. Often I came back with whatever she had gone in for in the first place, leaving her in peace to continue her chat. There is much talk nowadays about the decline of communities, urban isolation and its attendant evils. It's my belief that a good many ills in our society are directly attributable to the demise of the village shop, which not only acted as a conduit for news of all kinds, but also exercised an unofficial neighbourhood watch, as well as giving people a centre for social intercourse under the guise of merely supplying necessities like bread and milk.

Kathleen had three sons: Joe, Ronan and Raymond, all fine lads, but Ronan was the character. He was a particular favourite of my mother's, and visited her regularly from an early age. He started smoking at the tender age of nine, and on each visit, he would bring two cigarettes which he had filched from the shop, one for her and one for himself. This offering she would accept graciously, always making sure to return the favour before the visit ended. He always presented the spoils with a great flourish, despite their sometimes being flattened by a long sojourn in a pocket; and lit up with the injunction, "Don't tell my ma". To this my mother solemnly agreed, knowing full well that every night the tell-tale grains of tobacco would be shaken out of the pockets by Kathleen, who good-naturedly allowed the conspiracy to continue.

One day he came in full of news.

"Hi, Mrs. D'Arcy, wait'll you hear this. Me and the boys were down the back yesterday – don't tell my ma – trying to light a fag, when who do you think came along?"

"Who?" said Maureen, suitably agog.

"Soldiers," says Ronan, "three or four of them. One of them comes over and says in an England voice, 'Want a smoke boy?' Don't tell my ma."

"Of course not."

"So he offers us a cigarette, but none of the boys would take it. Finally I took it – don't tell my ma – and he pulls out a lighter. 'Want a light?' he says in an England voice. Now I'm not so good at lighting up, but I wouldn't let myself down, and I finally got it going. Don't tell my ma."

"Wasn't that kind of him?" said Maureen, not at all

sure how she was meant to react to the tale. Ronan withered her with a glance that would stop a funeral.

"Naw! He was looking something."

"What?" asked my mother, puzzled. "What did he want?"

This was Ronan's moment.

"Info!" says he.

Growing up in Dungannon in the '60s and '70s, the Troubles were second nature to children like Ronan. He roamed the town far and wide in the days when it was quite common to hear an explosion or two every day or so. I recall quite clearly counting seven in one day. When this happened one of the women in GHQ would muse, "I wonder where that one was?" and Kathleen would always make the same reply.

"Ronan will be in, in a minute; he'll know." And he always did.

He was the only person I ever knew who disliked Mona, and this came, I suspect, from the fact that she ribbed him mercilessly about coming to see her instead of my mother, and this he vehemently disputed. Searching one day for the ultimate insult with which to silence her forever, he spat out,

"You're the most ugliest in the house and I hate you!"

He was possessed of a green corduroy bomber jacket to which he was particularly attached, but sadly he began to grow out of it and soon it was literally coming apart at the seams. When this happened he would bring it down for my mother to sew. Soon it was more thread than fabric, but Ronan could not be disappointed, and much effort was expended in trying to keep it together for another while. One night my mother called into the shop for some fruit, and found Ronan perched on a high stool behind the counter.

"My ma's not well," he informed her, as she presented her selection of apples and oranges for pricing.

"Sure I'll pay you then," she told him.

Ronan looked from her to the fruit and considered his position; finally.

"Throw it agin the sewing," he said.

Ronan doesn't range the town now as he used to, and he probably doesn't smoke much either. He doesn't wear out bomber jackets, or mind the shop. A fine young man with a son of his own, he was stricken down some years ago with MS, and now he can barely get out of bed. He remained a favourite of my mother's to the day she died, and his illness saddened her to the core. We left the Donaghmore Road in 1974, just months before a bomb devastated it, ruining lives, families, houses and a whole community in one act of madness, but she never left it in her heart. She always talked about it and its people with regret and deep affection; Ronan she remembered with love.

The Spirit World

The pub on the Donaghmore Road was, in my mother's young days, owned by Paddy O'Neill, a handsome man, and if rumour is to be believed, one of his own most ardent admirers. To the children of the area (and others) he was known as Paddy Lovely, and it was not unusual to find a group of youngsters dancing on the pavement outside the front door and singing,

'Give me a pint of Lovely's stout, doo-dah, doo-dah,
A pint of Lovely's lovely stout, doo-dah, doo-dah-day!'

to the tune of *The Camptown Races*. Paddy however did not regard such serenades in a favourable light, and one day he made up his mind to complain to the parents of one urchin whom he recognised. The parents being out, the full wrath of a very disgruntled Paddy fell upon the child's sister, and in an era when a complaint from an adult was something to be taken seriously, the girl did her best to pacify him and ease the situation. Her embarrassment unfortunately led her into confusion and she stammered out,

"I'm sorry, Mr Beautiful, me ma and da's out, Mr Beautiful, but as soon as they come home I'll tell them, Mr Beautiful and they'll kill the wee skitter, so they will, Mr Beautiful."

The poor girl was completely at a loss as to why Paddy grew increasingly speechless with rage, while she continued to assure him that,

"He'll not get away with it, Mr Beautiful." It was only after he had stormed off with many a dire threat to return later that she realised what she had called him.

His wife Amy was a midwife, and one of my grandmother's best friends. To her she often confided her suspicions that her husband was not always a model of fidelity, and recounted the story of how she once followed him to Bundoran to catch him red-handed with his latest distraction. She spotted him coming towards her arm in arm with a lady, but as they drew level and she prepared to accost him she heard him muttering,

"Ignore her, ignore her, ignore her; the craythur's not wise, not wise, not wise. Don't encourage her now; the next thing is she'll be saying she's my wife; saying she's my wife. Walk on, I tell you, walk on." Amy was rendered speechless, while Paddy swept by with his conquest in tow.

This brings to mind an incident concerning another publican friend of ours, and his daughter, a close friend of my mother in her teens.

Susie was at this stage of her life a very beautiful girl, but very fond of her food. She also favoured heavy make-up and peroxide curls, and had developed an affected manner of speaking and what she considered a glamorous set of mannerisms, in the way that teenagers often do. She called herself 'Susie-wusie', and addressed all her friends in like mode; her fiancé was 'Frankie-wankie' which in more innocent times did not have today's unfortunate connotations, but which nonetheless did not go down well when she directed her letters to him thus while he was in the RAF!

One night Matt, her father, overheard a rather ribald comment directed at his daughter as she came down the stairs into the bar, and he made up his mind that forthwith she was to lose weight and tone down. He appointed himself her dietician, and his methodology was simple: she would be served the same portion of food as everyone else, but when she had swallowed only a few mouthfuls, he would remove her plate from in front of her saying,

"Enough! Enough! Enough!" with the result that Susie was permanently hungry. The effect of such drastic measures was to drive her eating underground.

My mother was at this time learning to play the piano, and Matt had arranged for her to come each evening after lessons and teach Susie what she had learned that day; in return she could stay to practise, since she did not at this time possess an instrument. This meant that each evening Susie had an uninterrupted couple of hours in the upstairs sitting-room without Matt hovering over her shoulder, and so, between scales and finger exercises, the girls dined off chocolate biscuits from under the sofa, buns and cakes from behind the chairs and on one memorable occasion, fish and chips from inside the piano. Matt never did figure out why the diet did not work, but he had to admit defeat and allow his daughter to resume normal eating habits.

The pub in my time was owned by John Daly, a publican of the old style, with bar apron, beard and pipe a fixture in his mouth. He and his wife Agnes, the light of his eyes, had one son, young John. These were the days before television became the scourge of pubs, and entertainment consisted of crack, darts and cards. Solo was the preferred game, and though John did not play, Agnes did, and he hated to see her lose. He would come round the bar to watch the game, puffing away contentedly if all was going well; but, though a man of few words, his disappointment if she was being beaten was plain to all.

One night, Wilf waited until all the hands were dealt and everyone considered their call.

"Mine's a spread misère," he announced laconically, probably the hardest hand of all to win, although as

Dan McGrew could testify, there are more ways than one to lose! With one mind and unspoken accord, every man around the table played to him, leaving him the clear victor and Agnes not within a hound's gowl of him. Many years later after Wilf had gone to England, I would meet people who had known him, and the talk would come round to the good old days.

"D'ye mind John Daly's?" someone would say; and this would inevitably be followed by,

"D'ye mind the night Wilf spread 'em?"

Of such things are legends made.

But John Daly kept a decent house, and was not like other publicans who were known to serve the contents of the drip-tray to anyone too far gone to notice; or the man whose mixtures were so unidentifiable that he was known as The Chemist.

There were some publicans who were their own best customers, like the man who bought and refurbished a pub, spending much time and money on it. Came the day when it was rumoured to be opening, and the town's pub cognoscenti gathered at the door around opening time. But nothing happened. After much knocking and hammering on doors, windows and other orifices, your man put his head out through the top window and addressed the throng.

"What d'yis want?"

"A drink; it's long after opening time."

"Yiz'll not get it here."

"Why? When are you opening?"

"I'm not. Did yiz think I bought the place for you?"

But publicans did not have it all their own way. Eugene Connolly, dying for a drink after the night before, managed to get in the back door of a well-known pub in Irish Street and waken the owner by shouting up the stairs to him.

"Givvus a drink, Andy."

"Go to Hell."

"I'm gasping."

"I don't care; I'm in bed. Come back later."

"I'll just get in beside you and wait," says Eugene, taking the stairs two at a time.

Wee Andy was down in the bar with a half one poured before you could say John Power's.

His opponent was a man who had never known defeat in encounters of this kind and, though often under the weather, was never lost for words. He had a tendency to go on the tear periodically, and one day he met a lady who was bold enough to remonstrate with him for his outrageous behaviour when under the influence.

"Away to Hell," he directed her, "and while you're at it, blacken your ass with Cherry Blossom."

Determined to do her duty though severely affronted she pursued, "You're a savage, but I'll pray for you."

"Don't bother," he told her. "You might be 'ating the altar rails, but yer woman you go to Mass with every morning could pray the ass off you."

His long-suffering wife had given up trying to make him mend his ways since the night she had waited up for him to return from a spree, intending to confront him one more time. She heard him ascend the stairs, and emerged from her bedroom just in time for him to prostrate himself at her feet with the words,

"Jesus meets his afflicted mother."

As the man says, there's no answer to that.

Of course, drink was not always bought over the counter in bona fide establishments, but often came in unmarked bottles from the mountains. Carrickmore was the scene of a near-scandal many years ago when it was reported that the children were going drunk to school. When closer investigation revealed that they were given a wee nip of a winter's morning to keep out the cold, nobody thought a thing of it.

Our neighbour, Alice, Mrs. McGeary to the children, came in every Christmas Eve to drink her annual sherry with my grandmother. Once she caused consternation by getting progressively drunker as the night wore on, even though no one refilled her glass (one was her limit), and it was clear that she hadn't even emptied it. She finished the evening in tears, telling my grandmother how lucky she was to have such a wonderful son as Wilfred, especially when it fell to him to see her safely over the hundred or so yards to her own front door, which she would never have managed on her own. On his return he found everyone agog at the spectacle, and explained,

"It was the wee drop of potin I slipped in her glass."

What he didn't add was that he had been topping it up all night unseen by anyone. Whatever effects Alice may have suffered in the morning, it's for sure she didn't attribute them to a hangover.

They say that when the potin is ready it is essential

to give the first run to the fairies, or the batch will be undrinkable. A glassful is run off and scattered on the ground with the words,

"Drink, little folk, drink." The remainder may then be bottled and used. What sensible distiller would fail to take such a basic precaution as this?

It may have been a drunken brawl induced by imbibing one such offering that my grandfather witnessed on his way home one night from his ceilidh at a neighbour's house. Walking along deep in thought, he was puzzled by the sound of angry exchanges from the other side of the hedge; looking over, he saw two groups of the good folk engaged in fisticuffs over the ownership of a small object which he made out to be a potstick. Quick as a flash, he whipped out his penknife, cut a switch from the hedge, fashioned it into the neatest wee potstick you ever saw, and threw in into the melée. There was instant silence, and suddenly my grandfather was alone in the moonlight. Wondering if he had imagined the whole episode, he strode on home.

But the fairies pay their debts, and they pay in kind; and when my grandfather woke the next morning, he could hardly get out of bed for the multitude of potsticks that had been laid upon his coverlet. In later years I have been moved to wonder why, if they could produce such a copious number of the things in the space of one night, they bothered to fight over the ownership of one; but as O'Casey says, a principle's a principle; or maybe they just enjoyed the exercise. Then again, as Chesterton observed,

———— ∞ ————

The Great Gaels of Ireland
Are the men that God made mad,
For all their wars are merry,
And all their songs are sad.

Maybe this is a trait we share with our otherworld cousins.

Soulmates

Dogs have always played an important part in our lives. One of my earliest memories is of a small black and white pointer-cross called Pincher, who could catch anything, be it tit-bit or toy, from wherever it was thrown, and no matter how unexpected its advent may have been. She was placid and quiet, perhaps a little lacking in spirit and personality, but the story goes that when I was brought home to Dungannon at six weeks old, she appointed herself my guardian and, from that moment on, allowed only well-known and trusted personnel to get within a hound's gowl of the carry-cot wherein I lay, stripping her teeth and growling at the unwelcome, a phenomenon that had never been observed before. Clearly a dog of discerning intellect, who was simply waiting for the right incentive to show her mettle.

My mother's favourite was Dash, a full-bred cocker spaniel and a gift from an old family friend. On a visit to Ballymulderg as teenagers, my mother and Mona were invited to admire Andy Derby's new puppies, and in common with most normal human beings, when faced with five or six mounds of face-licking, fat-bellied, wriggling fur, they were smitten.

"Take your pick," offered Andy, "If you want one. Any one you like, but if I was you, I'd take the wee one with the saddle."

The price? Nothing. For Andy was married to Minnie Johnston, whose family had been friends with the Larkins as far back as anyone could remember, and you don't charge friends, even if your bitch is a prize-winner and the sire has a sheaf of papers to prove his credentials. So the wee one with the saddle came to Dungannon, where, after a shaky start, he resided for the next seventeen years. He was a delicate pup, subject to convulsions, and a fussy feeder to boot, but an early diet of egg white and unconditional love soon brought him to maturity, although Wilf remained always slightly ashamed of him, since he wasn't macho enough to impress his mates. But he was a beautiful dog, with a rich coat and long silky ears, so long, that when he finally consented to eat from a bowl rather than being hand-fed, his ears had to be clipped up with a clothes-peg, to keep them out of his food.

Dash had two great pleasures in life: his daily walk and

chocolate. To ensure the former was not forgotten, he had a routine that varied only in length and complexity, depending upon the readiness of his humans. When he judged it time to go, he would go to the hallstand and get down his lead, bringing it to either Mona or my mother. Quite often, this produced the desired result, but sometimes the girls' state of readiness did not coincide with his. Then would follow a series of inducements, all connected with the outdoors – a scarf; gloves; a hat or cap; a shoe or two, all placed upon the chosen one's knee with a longing glance towards the door.

When my mother went to work in Coagh, he would watch for her every evening, knowing that she would bring him a tit-bit of chocolate or sweet of some kind, and when, having received his ration, any spare was put out of reach with the assurance, 'No more', Dash would take up position opposite the hiding-place and stare at it for several minutes, before slinking dejectedly off to lie down. He might not get any extra, but he wasn't going to allow them to believe he was fooled. He was generally a dog of honest nature, as he proved when accidentally locked in the kitchen one day with a dish of fresh pollen bought from the fish-man. After some time, my grandmother heard a scratch on the door and opened it to find Dash with one fish in his mouth, the rest carefully undisturbed and his prize untouched and unharmed, for he had the soft mouth of the gun-dog. He solemnly laid it at her feet and fixed her with that look that dog-owners know well, the one that makes getting a tear from a stone child's play. Needless to add, he was allowed to eat the fish. But sweets were a different matter altogether and if, on occasion, my mother failed to deliver the goods as soon as she walked through the door, he thought nothing of going to where her coat was hanging and helping himself from its pockets. This was probably his preferred course of action, since he never admitted his theft until only the wrappers were left, and then he would bring one into the kitchen, place it on the floor and walk around it in circles, finally settling down upon it for a well-earned nap.

In the course of time, Dash found true love in the form of Gyp, a Shetland Sheepdog, who followed Wilf home one night when he was working in Union Place. Efforts to find an owner proved fruitless, so Gyp remained, and soon the patter of tiny paws was heard about the house in the form of Cinders, Smudge and Dot, so called because she was all white except for one brown patch over one eye, and not, as everyone later thought, to match her sire's name. When the other dogs went to the happy hunting ground, Dash and Dot remained, Dot fixing her affections firmly on Mona and an old cricket ball, almost in equal measure. The ball and Dot were inseparable; she played with it incessantly and induced everyone of her acquaintance to throw it for her, including our landlord Tom, who was never known to be civil to anyone, human or brute, and all casual callers to the house, such as travellers, bread men and the like. If you didn't throw it far enough, she would not chase it; if she left it out of your reach, you only had to say, "Bring it over a bit," and it would materialise in your hand.

On one occasion it went missing, and Dot went into mourning, a serious state of affairs since she would neither eat nor drink, and exercise was out of the question. Replacements were bought and rejected. The neighbours brought offerings of their children's playthings, but to no avail. Susie Campbell arrived full of hope for she had found a ball identical in every respect to the missing one. It was presented and thrown with gusto; Dot leaped up and bounded after it – took one sniff and crept back to her place by the fire. It was not The One. Finally, just as the dog was beginning to be really ill, it was found on top of a cupboard where it had been put 'for safety'. I wonder how many precious things in life are lost through being put away for their own good! The family was assembled; the ball was thrown; breath was bated; but this time all was well. Dot seized upon the treasure with an excess of joy usually associated with the release of hostages; she whined and quivered from nose to tail with happiness, and for several days would not play with the thing, but lay and nursed it between her front paws in case it should get away from her again.

Dash had no interest in the ball, but it provided him with additional negotiating power when the occasion demanded. There was a chair in the kitchen with an old cushion on it, reserved for Dash as he grew older. In the manner of all teenage delinquents, Dot would sometimes claim it first and lie eyeballing her father and daring him to evict her, while she growled ferociously at him. This he would endeavour to do by catching the cushion in his teeth and pulling, or going round the back and pushing with his nose; but though he was too much of a gentleman to tip her right off, he never gave up hope that she would do the decent thing and move. She never did and, one night, driven to extreme measures, he procured the ball and bounced it across the floor. Dot was off the chair faster than you could say starting pistol, leaving Dash in possession, a manoeuvre which served him well on many a subsequent occasion.

Many years after Dot died, we found the ball in the bottom of an old trunk, and it still had the power to bring tears to any of us who were there. My mother always said that the very people who love dogs most are those who should never keep them, for their passing is so painful to us, and is probably the one loss in life that we never fully recover from. She was right; yet as Axel Munthe says, we do not just love *a* dog, we love *the* dog; and once you have experienced their unconditional love, you can never bear to be without it, no matter what the drain on your emotions.

My dog was also the gift of a friend. Her mother was Salty, a cross between a Labrador and a Springer Spaniel, her father a Border Collie. I met her at three weeks old and was besotted. She was all black, save for three white hairs on her chest, which she never lost, and, uncommonly, blue eyes. Her foster-mother, Joan, called her Titch-bitch, because she was the runt of the litter, last out of the basket and last back in, and therefore often the last to be fed. The night before she was due to be dropped off at my house, I lay awake and reflected upon the enormity of what I had taken on: muddy feet, hairs on the sofa, walks every day, grooming, training, vaccinations, loss of free time, expense, responsibility, and I quailed. The family had spent the evening choosing a name for the new arrival; Royal babies have not had so much attention given to their nomenclature since the first syllable of recorded time. We rejected anything 'ordinary', yet did not want anything gimmicky. We wanted to be original, but not eccentric; and we wanted something that would 'suit'. At that time we were all reading Tolkien's masterpiece *The Lord of the Rings*, and eventually, everything else having been rejected, my aunt said jokingly,

"What about Gollum?"

Now for anyone who has read the book, the choice defies explanation, and for anyone who hasn't, there can be no explanation, for to name an adorable black puppy after a sneaky, slimy, treacherous and ugly creature is a conceit of the rarest kind, yet it seemed right. And so she was named, this being who was to define my life for almost seventeen years, and who still inhabits my dreams and my memory. She was the size of a good spaniel, but favoured the Labrador in general appearance, though she had the more slender muzzle of the collie and its plumy tail. She had the thickest, glossiest coat imaginable with a curious kind of saddle effect along her spine that made her look as if she had been trace-clipped. As I have said, she was all black, a circumstance which prompted one of my aunt's famous Mona-isms, for Mona had the gift of the Irish bull which produced such gems as,

"This room's too warm; what we need is a cold heat-er," or, searching for a container in which to carry milk for a picnic,

"There's an empty bottle here with a wee drop in it."

Admiring Gollum one day she remarked,

"We've never had a black dog before and she's all black. The only thing white about her is her teeth and her wee pink tongue."

Like Dot, she loved to play ball, and could catch like a professional cricketer. She was fast, nimble and loved a challenge. She was the cleverest dog we ever had, always one step ahead of us, never outwitted in play and with a nice line in flirting, whereby if the person whose attention she wanted was otherwise engaged, she made a great show of lavishing affection on someone else in such a way that the point could not be missed. She discovered early on how to close the cover of any book I tried to read in her presence, and made it her business to search your pockets if there was a biscuit secreted anywhere about your person. She was also a fussy eater and, as a puppy went for a whole week without anything, determinedly rejecting everything she was offered, including cereal, porridge, brown bread and milk and every conceivable form of commercial concoction, until I thought she would surely starve to death. But Mona saved the day. I came home from work to find Gollum in the kitchen wolfing down something indescribable, and licking her whiskers after it.

"What…" I began.

Mona was beaming seraphically.

"Heinz baby dinners," she said. "She loved it."

———— ∞ ————

And for the next few months, the dog would sit by the cooker while the food was heated (in a saucepan of hot water), then move to the sink where the tin was opened, and then wait until it reached the correct temperature, too hot being unacceptable (to Mona). The dish would be licked clean every time, before being tossed about the room like a Frisbee, either in celebration of the quality of the repast, much as the Greeks break glasses, or in protest that there was no more.

Beef casserole was her favourite.

She did graduate to other things, but to the day she died at almost seventeen, she steadfastly refused to eat dog food, and all my bulk buys and special offers were trundled into work and passed on to those whose dogs knew their place. Dog biscuits, however, were preferred to human ones, and in adulthood her diet consisted mainly of sliced turkey (which my mother would warm in her hands if she thought it too cold), Bonios and raw carrots. In later life, she enjoyed real beef casserole, but only if gin had been added during cooking, and chicken breast, without sauce.

This diet kept her in rude good health and she was only sick twice, but both times almost fatally. A colleague lost her dog to parvo virus, and two days later Gollum succumbed; I am still convinced that in some way I carried the infection home. She was very poorly, and we considered it too late even to ring the vet, but my mother was a fighter and a woman of strong if sometimes unorthodox faith, so she produced a relic of

St. Martin de Porres, who had the reputation of being an animal-lover, with the words,

"Right, St. Martin, let's see what you can do," and proceeded to rub the relic on the dog's head and exhort us all to pray for her.

Whether it was her unusual mode of address, or her own deep conviction that "He'll do the trick," or our patent distress at the prospect of losing, at eight months old, something dear and precious to us all, I cannot say; but St. Martin or someone heard our plea and a couple of hours later the dog was able to stand alone, and even licked a baby dinner (probably beef casserole) which I fed her with the tears tripping me. An hour or two after that she made a go for the ball, and we knew all was well.

When she was eight, I took her for a check-up for she had been unable to keep water down, and was told she had developed pyometria, common enough for a maiden bitch who had not been spayed, but potentially fatal. I left her in for an operation, wondering, not for the first time, how such small creatures can elicit such huge reactions in human beings. For the waiting rooms are redolent of anxiety any time you go, and the matter-of-factness of the staff contrasts with the gnawing fear inside you as you nonchalantly pat the patient's head and walk jauntily out, pretending it doesn't bother you, and wondering if your legs will get you to the door.

But this episode had a happy ending. We went to collect her next morning, and she wouldn't come out of the cage. I was allowed to go in to call her, for she would

not respond to the vet's blandishments, or his calls of
"Gollum! Gollum honey." *Honey* was disgusted at the
standard of her lodgings – a cold metal cage with newspaper – newspaper! – on the floor. Where was her raised
platform to keep her out of the draught? Her floor cushion? Her rug? That it was clean and practical for a surgery impressed her not at all, and she finally emerged,
still woozy from the anaesthetic, but in high dudgeon,
and made straight for us, coming to a halt against the
knee of my other best friend, Issy, for she was weaker
than she thought. She was brought home in triumph
to a new bed, placed in front of the fire, and a return to
hand feeding with slivers of her favourite delicacies.

"Sure she needs to be cooked like an egg," observed
my mother, "And she'll never look behind her." And so
it proved.

At fifteen she developed a mammarian tumour, but
we were advised against operating on the basis that she
was unlikely to survive the anaesthetic, and in any case
would probably die before it got too big, as she was
already alive over the odds, but the vet did not favour
euthanasia as she was still in good fettle. But she was
never predictable and, though deaf and blind, was able
to enjoy a good quality of life, even extending her diet
to include cheese and potato cakes and baked potatoes.
The tumour continued to grow and eventually broke
down, making a visit to the vet inevitable, the same vet
who had kept her alive before and, perhaps moved by
her spirit (she still tried to nip his hand as he examined
her!), he decided to operate. At sixteen she came through

a major trauma and survived. The vet had never seen such a massive tumour, or an elderly dog make such a recovery. For three nights we sat up with her, Issy and I setting up camp beds in the living room to watch in case she pulled out the drain, burst her stitches, or needed anything, a small service in our eyes, but one which elicited the greatest compliment either of us has ever received. We were telling a friend of this episode, and he remarked,

"You deserve a dog." What greater accolade could anyone want?

But time and tide wait for neither man, woman nor dog, and finally the Grim Reaper called time. Gollum had been unable to lap water for several months, so Issy poured water into her mouth from a jug, and her appetite was as good as ever; but one Thursday, she would neither eat nor drink. Her gums had become inflamed and we guessed she was in pain, but she was gutsy and never complained. So many times in the past, I had glibly said how one must be brave, think of the dog, let her go at the end rather than prolong her suffering, yet I defy anyone who has had to face the decision to have one's dog put to sleep to tell me they did it without their whole soul in turmoil, and their heart wrung beyond endurance. In the end it was Issy who said what had to be said and gave me the courage to do what I had to do. And even in death, Gollum showed what an unusual dog she was.

I had made up my mind to call the vet on Monday morning, my day off. On Sunday night as I settled

Gollum down for what I knew would be her last night, she allowed me to cuddle her, and just as I was about to leave her, gave two sharp barks. I told myself she was saying she was ready to go. The following morning, as I waited for the vet to arrive, we had a phone call from the hospital. My uncle, who had been ill for many months with lung cancer, had taken a turn for the worse – could anyone come? I knew then that I would mourn two friends that day, because for the past few months, Wilf had been measuring his state of health against the dog's, so much so that we had not told him of her deterioration, and had no intention of telling him of her death. When we arrived to visit him, his first question was always,

"How's the wee dog?" and he always related his own suffering to hers, complaining about getting older, stiffer, becoming dependent; and of course, of the cancer they shared. And now, I knew they would depart together.

Alan came, the same vet who had removed the tumour, and confirmed our fears. Her small body was cool, where it was always warm, and she lay in my arms with no attempt to move. He gave her a first injection to make her sleep, and left us alone for a few moments, then gave her another to stop her heart.

"Are you sure she can't feel anything?" I had to be sure.

"Nothing," he replied, "She's almost gone."

But not quite. She raised her head and barked three times, and then was still.

"That's very unusual," said Alan. She was an unusual dog.

I suppose we focus on the inane when we face great grief. I remember thinking, as I watched Alan give the lethal shot, what beautiful hair he had. I wonder was I thinking of Gollum's beautiful coat, and how I would never brush it again. I stroked it until she was quite cold, wrapped her in her rug, and left for the hospital. Less than two hours later, I said goodbye to Wilf, and as I walked out of the hospital to go and find an undertaker, I firmly believed that somewhere, a fit and healthy Wilf was whistling to a small black dog and saying,

"My life on you, Gollum, isn't it great to be free of the ould pain?"

You never understand anything until you experience it yourself, grief more than any other emotion. Love, Jealousy, Fear, Regret, we feel in differing degrees throughout our lives, but loss of a loved one takes you by the throat and shakes the heart out of you. That day proved what I had begun to suspect when Mona died, and to be fairly sure of when my mother followed her: what we miss, is not someone we love, but someone who loves us. We meet new people as time goes by and some of those we will bestow our affections upon; but the loss of the certainty of being loved in return is hard to bear.

But life does go on, and now there's Meg, a beautiful Border Collie, whose life revolves around cuddles and – a ball! We got her, at Issy's prompting, when Gollum was still with us, and there's no doubt that she helped ease the passing. She is love on four feet, would die for a hug, will eat anything she is given and much that she should not, and will one day play for Europe, such is her skill with a football. She has not taken Gollum's place, but occupies entirely her own space in our affections. She is entirely different in nature, but with her own sense of fun, is much more biddable, but just as manipulative, in the nicest possible way! It is good to have a young dog again, and to watch her race along a beach or through a forest park, and fly like a black and white arrow after a stick or ball; and if we are privileged to have her into old age, that will be good too. I showed her Gollum's collar one day, and she lay down and whined, then came to me for a hug. Who says dogs don't think?

No catalogue of canine friends would be complete without one who isn't mine at all but in whom I have a small claim. A very good friend had been ill, and we wondered if a dog of her own would cheer her up. It had to be a bitch and it had to be small; she had always had a yen for a King Charles Spaniel, but having scanned the papers for news of likely breeders with pups and drawing a blank, we decided to rescue or adopt if possible. But no joy.

"Hello? I'm calling about the puppy, free to good home…"

"Aye, lovely dog, good-natured, mother's a pedigree Lab, good with kids…"

"What's it crossed with?"

"Next door's Rottweiler." Click.

"USPCA? Do you have any pups for rehoming?"

"Not this week."

Finally I rang the dog warden in Dungannon, thinking he would only have dogs awaiting collection, or adults who might not be suitable.

"I'm looking for a bitch puppy, and preferably a small breed. And I wondered if you'd know…"

"How about a nine-week-old King Charles Spaniel?"

After I'd picked myself up off the floor and downed a double brandy, I said, faintly,

"A what?"

A woman who bred the little fellows was afraid one of her bitches had been playing away from home, and the three gorgeous pups she produced were not full-bred; but being a responsible dog-owner, had asked our warden Mervyn, to try to get homes for them.

"I'll be there in a minute."

When I arrived one had been adopted, leaving a wheaten-coated dog and a tawny bitch. This latter burst out of the kennel, walking over her brother's head as she did so, and hurled herself upon us. It was hard to tell the difference between nose and tail, for she insisted on turning complicated somersaults in between licking us to death. It was not open to debate, though we played hard to get for a minute or two, God knows why, except perhaps that we were tempted to take them both, only Mervyn assured us he had someone lined up for the little dog. So in she went to a cardboard box, inside a paper-lined car boot, and off we drove to Portadown, me with my hand inside the box for the dog to chew on to keep her from getting nervous. And then the name game began again. Toffee? Someone at work has a dog called that. Honey? So-and-so's dog is called that. Goldie? Too ordinary. Guinevere? Get real! And then I looked at the morsel in the back, with its four white feet and plumy tail, its golden-syrup body and white muzzle, its tiny pin-sharp teeth busy on my hand, while its soft tongue licked the wounds to show there was nothing personal, and I thought, she's good enough to eat; and I knew there was only one name for her.

"Fudge," I said.

As soon as we got her home, we were terrified that we had done the wrong thing. Supposing Marie didn't really want a dog of her own? Maybe we had taken too much on ourselves, maybe she wasn't ready for one, maybe, maybe, maybe. The family was assembled in the garden, Marie was due home from work, everyone was tense; everyone that is except for Fudge, who spent the time getting acquainted with us by climbing all over us and licking and biting with equal abandon. Marie approached; we closed ranks around The Surprise; we pulled back.

"Oh look," she said, matter-of-factly. We waited.

"Who's going to run me into town to buy her a basket?"

From that day on she is undisputed mistress of all she surveys. She doesn't disobey commands, she ignores them. She swears like a trooper when discommoded, eg. when asked to vacate the best seat in the house because the visitors have to sit on the floor; and will fight all comers for her ration of vittles. She will threaten the hand that tries to remove a twig from her coat, but treats like royalty the girl who manicures her and trims her golden locks. She will defend her rocking chair against any passer-by, and will, if not closely monitored, walk across the table in search of sweet stuff, once being caught in the act of swallowing whole a huge slice of fruit cake, python-fashion; and she will kill for ice-cream.

But she will also leap on the bed in the mornings and turn upside down to have her belly tickled, a position which flattens her large spaniel ears into a likeness of Gizmo the Gremlin; fly through the air from couch to chair in order to be first to welcome you into the house; and wriggle from her particular corner of the sofa until she has got her head exactly where she wants it – on your knee.

When she misbehaves badly enough we threaten to call Mervyn to come and repossess her, a threat which is also made to Marie when Fudge's legion of admirers feel aggreived that she should be chastised!

And my claim on her? I was the first to pick her up the day she hurtled out of her temporary shelter in Dungannon's Council dog pound.

Lie over Da...

When my mother first came to Dungannon she made the acquaintance of an elderly lady called Miss Downey. She lived alone; kept herself to herself, and nothing much was known about her. When she died at a fairly advanced age, the neighbours scanned the papers for news in the death notice of relatives, kin and so on, but no death notice was found. There was, however, an entry under HUGHES, and closer perusal revealed that the details matched the dead woman's exactly. Was there a clerical error? A drunken typesetter? Or better still, A Story? There was a story.

As a young woman, Miss Downey had been betrothed to a local farmer, an arranged match, common enough at the time, suitable to both families and more or less acceptable to the two parties. On the appointed day, the priest turned up, the guests turned up, the bride turned up, but there was no sign of the groom. After a tense interval in church a delegation of two or three menfolk was dispatched to see if an accident had befallen him on the way thither, but they were amazed to find him alive and well and out making hay with his brother. With no little annoyance they upbraided him for his failure to show up for his nuptials. He was mildly chagrined.

"Jaysus, I forgot!" he exclaimed, turning to his brother. "Here, go you."

Naturally his brother declined to oblige, pointing out the obvious difficulties, and he was eventually prevailed upon to get cleaned up and go. At last the happy couple was united in holy wedlock, and since these were the days before lavish receptions lasting all day and well into the evening, or exotic honeymoons with tight schedules to be met, there was no real harm done, except to the bride's ego. Late but wedded, the pair returned to the farm which was to be their home. When the time came for them to retire to the bridal chamber it was quite dark. Mr Hughes led Miss Downey to a large, sparsely furnished bedchamber containing a large double bed, to which he conducted her without ceremony, pausing only to say,

"Lie over, Da, and make room for Downey."

Needless to say, room was not needed, and the old gentleman's sleep was not disturbed again. Miss Downey collected her belongings, returned to Dungannon and, from that day onwards never acknowledged her husband or her connection with him, until her death, maybe sixty years later.

Marriage and matchmaking was of course a serious affair, and the story is told of a family who had a daughter to get off their hands, but not much to offer her in the way of a dowry. Undaunted, they would invite a prospective suitor to the house, a small structure, of single storey, with windows only to the front, and these small ones. When he had been plied with the best they could offer in food, and perhaps a drop of potin, the father would say,

"Mary, would you bring in the cattle."

Primed and ready, the girl would dutifully drive their one cow round and round the house until the viewers had lost count of the number of passes. Then the mother would say,

"Has she never the cows in yet?"

The success of this ploy is not recorded, but nowadays the RSPCA would be looking into allegations of bovine abuse.

My uncle was a great admirer of womankind, but never to the point where he wanted to be shackled to one for life. He was, as they say, fond of a drink, and would often aver that his preference was for the blonde with the black skirt (a bottle of Guinness) above any living woman. When he grew tired of being asked why he never married he would give one of two answers:

"Why marry and make one woman miserable, when I can stay single and make dozens happy?" or "Many's the girl I was in love with, but none of them would marry me when I was drunk, and I wouldn't take any of them when I was sober."

And to emphasise the folly of such things he would break into song: *By the Bright Silvery Light of the Moon*, or *She Was Very Peculiar for Eighteen Years Old*, two cautionary tales of young men being duped by a pretty face.

But not everyone shared his cynicism. A friend of ours had a lifelong love affair with her husband, though to be sure it started inauspiciously enough. Married in Dungannon, they were to honeymoon in Dublin, staying with friends of the groom. Arrived in the smoke, Jimmy was taken out for a celebratory drink by the man of the house, while his wife entertained Annie. But one drink led to another and the two returned later than planned, unaware that the bride had spent the intervening hours working herself up into a fury at being thus made to wait. When Jimmy entered the bedroom he was met, not by a blushing bride eager to please her new husband, but by a raging fury who set upon him with a will, punching, kicking, biting and swearing she would have to be dug out of him, finally ripping the sweater he was wearing to shreds. He was black and blue by the time her fury was spent. Whether to make up for this lapse or not, she spent the rest of her life declaring her undying passion for him, avowing that she loved him 'from his wee bald head to his wee short legs.' Totally devoted to you. Many years later she revealed that she had kept the sweater (what was left of it) to remind her of her rage, and deter her from a repeat performance. No doubt Jimmy guarded it with his life too. She and her sister once nearly came to blows, each insisting that she had married the best man in Ireland; finally they agreed, in the interests of harmony, that they had married the two best men in Ireland; compromise is all.

Advice to young women was never lacking, even if sometimes conflicting. One lady used to say, "You'll meet your fate, even if you live in a bandbox," while another insisted, "If you don't show, you won't sell." Another friend who favoured rather outlandish dresses ("Mutton come lamb," said Maureen) explained her penchant for frills and flounces thus: "It was the bow that got the master." The arcane significance of the phrase escaped me for years until one day I did the sensible thing and asked my mother, "What on earth did she mean by that?" Maureen favoured me with a look that could stop a funeral and returned, with a brevity that spoke volumes, "She married a teacher."

Courtship rituals took various forms. An elderly couple recalled fondly how they used to meet in a friend's house, and sit on opposite sides of the fire clodding wee bits of turf at each other as a sign of affection; while another pair, having been diplomatically left alone by friends who suspected that love was in the air, were discovered after a decent interval gazing into each other's eyes and happily discussing the price of hens.

My mother was scathing about many of the partners chosen by her friends. "I wouldn't court him for spite," she said of one; of another, "I wouldn't take him on a string of herrings to make a dozen." At best she held the view that love is blind but marriage is an eye-opener, and would advise me and my friends, "Girls, if you can afford to do without a man, don't bother; they're only good for the oul' spondulicks." She had many tales to tell of marriages made anywhere but in Heaven. There was the couple who admitted they married each other for money, and were most indignant when they found out they were both penniless; the man who, as he left the church, asked his bride to lend him the crown he had just given her (...*gold and silver, tokens of all I possess...*) to buy the best man a drink; or the father-in-law who advised the groom on his wedding day, "Enjoy yourself today, son, for she comes of a terrible long-lived family."

Upon being told of the impending marriage of a couple who had walked out for an inordinately long time, she remarked, "Long sickness is death at last," and then went on to recount the tale of two lovers who had courted for many years without any proposal being made, when the woman felt compelled to hint at a more permanent arrangement.

"John," says she, "The neighbours are all saying that we're about to get married."

"Ach catch yerself on, Maggie," chuckled John, taking the pipe from his grizzled lips to allow himself the luxury of a good spit. "Sure who the hell would take either of us now?"

Marriage could be an expensive business, then as now. One man, known to be near, went to see the parish priest to get an estimate of the cost. Knowing the man's reputation, the priest asked him how much money he had.

"Ten bob, Father," he was told. Jokingly, the priest tut-tutted and shook his head.

"Ah, you wouldn't have enough there," he told him.

"Sure marry me as far as it goes and it'll do rightly," says our man.

Romance is never quite dead, however. At a wedding in Pomeroy the priest asked the bride,

"Do you take this man…?"

Receiving no reply he tried again, thinking she was overcome by nerves, but at the second attempt she burst into tears and blurted out,

"I can't go through with it!"

There was consternation in church, murmuring and head-shaking among the guests. Astounded, the priest asked her why, at which point the best man stepped forward and said,

"Because she loves me, and I love her."

When the ensuing uproar was quieted, the groom gallantly stepped aside, and the wedding continued, with the friends changing places. It's comforting to know that sometimes the best man does win.

Coincidences happen with marriage as in all walks of life. An inspector arrived one day at a small country school near The Loup to put the pupils through their paces. To one particularly difficult question, only one child, a girl, knew the answer. The inspector was intrigued, and told the class that in all his years as a school inspector only one other child, a boy in Magherafelt, had correctly answered his question. Many years later the boy and girl met and married and became my grandparents.

But not all marriages in my family were happy. Perhaps the most unfortunate was that of Mary Larkin, a cousin of my grandmother's, who, around the turn of the century, was courted by a Mr Walsh, a man of good breeding and impeccable lineage whose family were landowners, farmers and hoteliers. It was regarded as a brilliant match, and Mary's wedding present from her father was a magnificent pony and trap, the sports car of the day. It was not long before Mary was to learn that Walsh had fallen on hard times, and was, to put it mildly, on his uppers. He was deeply in debt and the suspicion began to grow on her that he had married her as a way out of his difficulties. Now the Larkins' most notable characteristic was family pride, so Mary settled his debts so as not to be associated with any hint of scandal; but having done so, she loaded all her personal effects onto the trap and made the short journey home, informing her husband that all communication between them must cease from that time on. Divorce in such a family at such a time was unthinkable, but she maintained her resolve and lived out her life under her parents' roof. As she lay on her deathbed he attempted to see her; her sister announced his visit with,

"Walsh is downstairs."

But Mary declined to see him. Even in death she would not acknowledge him. She is buried with her parents, who predeceased her, and whose names and dates appear in full on the stone that marks their grave. Her inscription reads simply:

Also their daughter, Mary Elizabeth.

Dr Who

He was known to some as a spoiled priest, one who had completed a term of study at Maynooth seminary without actually entering Holy Orders, being regarded by many as somehow not quite 'right', as if refusing to answer the call of God, or being unable to do so, left one in some manner marked for life. It was said that his health failed; in later years I wondered about the possibility of a 'nervous breakdown'. Now I guess he just did not have a vocation, and chose instead to plough a lone and lonely furrow in the world, which he nonetheless rejected in his own peculiar way. Perhaps rejected is not quite the right word; he accepted some of its strictures readily enough; others he simply ignored. Time meant nothing to him; he held no steady employment, slept throughout the day and wandered the town and country by night afoot or on his bicycle. He had a number of calling-houses, of which ours was one, where he would arrive no earlier than eleven at night, and depart therefrom as dawn broke, having spent the night in converse, as with us, or reading and meditating in houses where his hosts went off to bed and left him. My mother never did that. I discovered as I grew older that although she was prepared to tolerate his visits, she did not trust him; as it turned out, she was right.

The world knew him as Gerald. We always called him Dr Who.

That he was allowed to come and go at such unusual hours was a direct result of my grandmother's insistence,

"No one will insult a guest in my house."

And because he was not told to keep to a reasonable time-scale on his first visit, the pattern became established. As a child I found it quite natural to have him arrive as I went off to bed; and at weekends I stayed up to listen in to the conversation, which ranged from the excruciatingly boring to the rivetingly interesting. For he could talk at length on any subject you might introduce – tea, in all its manifestations from crop to cup; ghosts and the supernatural; the animal kingdom; politics; history; and religion was of course a favourite. He was astonishingly well read; and like all genuine lovers of learning, was always keen to acquire more. I well remember my own small triumph, which at the tender age of seven years brought me no little pleasure. I was one of his greatest admirers, for he never treated me like a child, but accorded me the same importance as my elders. It was his habit always to address everyone in the room by name as he began a story,

"Wilfred, Maureen, Mona, Aideen…" In an era when children were seen but not heard, much less spoken to, I was an equal.

My grandmother always bought me comics, one of which had a page of *Strange Facts From the Animal World*, wherein I read that the horn of the rhinoceros is neither horn nor bone, nor yet ivory, but consists of masses of hair. I was fascinated by this (I was that sort of child) and hastened to share my knowledge with Dr Who. He immediately disputed the claim, but I maintained my stance, and a standoff resulted, amicable on his part, less so on mine. Several weeks later I was in the local shop two doors up when a voice spoke behind me.

"Aideen! I owe you an apology."

Several heads turned towards the Doctor, for it was he.

"Following our discussion the other night about the rhinoceros horn," he continued, "I went and checked it up. You were absolutely right. I am very sorry to have disagreed with you."

My honour vindicated, we were back on the best of terms.

He was that sort of man.

❦

His eccentricities were innumerable, and he was not averse to admitting to them. He recounted how, settling down to read before bed, as he always did, taking in something in Irish, Latin and English, he suddenly felt the room growing chill. He lived with his sister, or at least they shared a house, but as she operated to a more or less normal timetable, they rarely saw each other and were not on the best of terms. He never used her name.

"SHE had let the fire go out," he told us, "So I looked around for an extra coat."

He found a coat belonging to her, which he put on under his own jacket, over his vest, shirt and sweater, with his overcoat on top, but was still cold. He took the heavy chenille tablecloth from the table and wrapped it about his shoulders, but was still cold. He found a woollen rug over a chair and, filling a hot water bottle, which he rested on his knees, he tucked this in also. He added a scarf, his cap and a thick pair of gloves, and then - success? No!

"Maureen, Mona, Aideen, Wilfred – there was still a draught! Just at the Adam's apple where the collar and the scarf did not quite meet. The only place where a draught could find ingress!"

"Surely to God," interposed my uncle, "You didn't undo all them tartles and start again?"

"But no!" cried he with the air of one who has discovered a cure for the common cold. "I fixed it! I stuffed in the handkerchief!"

"After that," says Wilf, "I wouldn't have the energy to turn the pages."

He and Wilf enjoyed a very peculiar relationship. Wilf did not approve of him for several reasons: he wouldn't work in a fit; he was a bit of a 'ginny'; he was namby-pamby. But he admired his intellect, enjoyed disputation with him, and took a perverse pleasure out of threatening to go to bed and leave him alone with Mona, for it was widely acknowledged that she was one of the main reasons he came visiting. It was to improve his argumentative powers with him that Wilf decided to read the Bible, for Gerald was fond of Scriptural references. Like many Catholic households of the day we did not possess a Bible of our own, so Wilf persuaded my mother to go to Smithfield in Belfast to buy one. The trip lived in her memory as one long nightmare. She was wearing high strappy sandals that cut into her feet (*bloody dog muzzles*, according to Wilf), and they walked the length and breadth of Belfast when Smithfield failed to provide what they came for. It rained incessantly all day, but Wilf on a quest was like a pig going to hoke, and would not be gainsaid. When no Bible was found, he decided to buy me a present, and retraced his steps until he acquired the teddy bear he had seen earlier in the day, and all this without a tea break. They finally made it back to the station where my mother insisted on sitting down in the buffet and resting her feet, where she ordered some much needed tea and sandwiches, while Wilf went to check the train times. She had just managed to extricate her aching limbs from their instruments of torture when Wilf hailed her from the door.

"Hurry up, the last train for Dungannon is about to leave!"

She never moved so fast, or with such reluctance.

A Bible was eventually procured from a good Presbyterian friend, and Wilf read it from cover to cover, much to my grandmother's chagrin, for he insisted upon referring to her as he read.

"Mother! What does begat mean?"

"Don't annoy me, Wilf."

"Mother! There's a man here who wants to marry his sister! This is a bad book."

"God forgive you, boy."

"Mother! What does W.H.O.R.E. spell?"

"Don't come over talk like that in my house!"

"But it must be all right, it's in the Bible."

"Mother…"

"I don't want to know, Wilf!"

Altogether a more innocent age!

At any rate, he became as fascinated by his studies as Service's Salvation Bill, and turned into a regular Bible scholar.

Gerald's taste in food was as eccentric as his attempts to keep warm. He was an early advocate of the food combining principle, and recked not what he ate as long as it contained the requisite vitamins and nutrients, which he deemed necessary to his physical well being.

By his own account, he was left to his own devices in a house where he was a frequent visitor after the household had retired for the night, and during the small hours he became peckish. It was a country house, where heating and cooking alike were taken care of by a large range in the kitchen. Finding the fire out and being thereby deprived of a means of cooking, Gerald went rummaging in the larder. He took a baking bowl, poured in some cereal, milk and sugar; added currants and raisins and dried soup mixture; added suet for the fat content, and bound the whole lot with treacle.

"And did you eat it?" Wilf wanted to know.

"I did, Wilf, every bit."

"I wouldn't give it to a calf," opined my uncle.

"It wasn't bad," Gerald assured him, "Though I thought later it might have been better without the treacle."

One man's meat…

But he was partial to sweet things as well. He told us how 'She' used to buy tins of biscuits and secrete them around the house. He then made it his business to discover her 'hidey-holes' and abstract his favourites, which he would bring to our house wrapped in a football coupon and tied around with string, usually only one or two, to be eaten with his cup of tea which he would order, when he was ready, with the incantation,

"Maureen, Mona, Aideen – who's on duty tonight?"

Or sometimes it would be a glass of H_2O (thus I learned my first scientific formula!), served in a glass of specific thickness, neither too fine nor too coarse. When we finally found one to his liking, my mother put it away at the back of the cupboard and allowed no one else to use it in case it got broken, "For I couldn't be bothered with that palaver every time he wants a drink."

One night he cycled farther than he intended, and was tired on the way home.

"The only thing that kept me going was the slice of walnut cake I had hidden under the pillow."

He watched me eating a bun one night and remarked, "Aideen, that looks delicious. Where did you get it?"

"In Tommy O'Neill's," I replied.

Wilf regarded him over the stump of a Woodbine.

"Would you like one?" he asked.

Receiving an answer in the affirmative, he handed Gerald sixpence to go and buy himself one, which he did, and proceeded to tuck into it with great relish. After watching for a moment or two, Wilf removed the butt from his mouth and pronounced the immortal words:

"Would you not be better to take the paper off?"

I wondered why he never gave Wilf his change.

But there was a dark side to Doctor Who that only became clear after long acquaintance. One night Mona asked him why he never slept at night, a casual question, expecting some glib answer.

"I can't," he replied. "I'm cursed."

He then embarked on a tale, which I wasn't allowed to

listen to at the time, but later discovered the gist of it to be as follows.

After graduating, he went to London where he secured a good post with the Education Department, taking lodgings with a family who were distantly related to his own. He soon developed a fondness for the daughter of the house, Mary, which was not reciprocated, and this he found impossible to accept. He took to following her around, becoming in fact a stalker, before such terms were fashionable, and he soon observed that she was very active in the affairs of her local church, being a member of the altar society, the choir and a very active fund-raiser. It was these activities, he persuaded himself, that diverted her attention away from him, and the cause of all this was, he decided, the young curate, who was in fact a friend of the family and often called at the house. Knowing in his heart that it was false, he accused Mary and the priest of having an affair, at first verbally, and then, one night, after a lengthy campaign of innuendo and rumour, pouring out his spleen in ten notepads which he sent to the priest, and another lengthy document which he sent to the Bishop.

The following evening he was coming through the hallway when he saw the lady of the house admit the parish priest, who was holding in his hand the aforementioned notebooks.

"I knew the game was up," he told us.

"What did you feel?" asked my mother. "Weren't you afraid?"

— ∞ —

"I didn't give a damn," he replied, "I knew I had ruined them."

Mary and the priest were both on the edge of a breakdown; she had given up her job, and the young priest felt he must leave the parish, for there are always some who prefer to believe the worst; yet he knew that to do so might seem like an admission of guilt. Gerald, of course, had to quit the house and his job, and soon after returned to Ireland.

"And that is why I cannot sleep," he said. "I will never sleep until I write and beg their forgiveness. I will do it someday; but not yet."

"What became of Mary and the priest?" my mother wanted to know.

"She married, I believe; he went to another parish."

"But you knew none of this was true?" My mother half-believed he had been subject to delusions.

"Of course," he said, "But it didn't matter. I wanted to hurt them."

Much later, we discovered how bad an enemy he could be.

Two circumstances combined to make his visits to us less comfortable for him, both, ironically, of his own making.

We were given a black and tan terrier puppy whom I instantly named Sooty, a complete and utter tearaway who was ungovernable and untameable, partly because he spent most of his time enclosed in a small garden, there being nobody to exercise him, for I was too young and my grandmother had fallen victim to cancer and was being nursed around the clock by my mother and Mona. One day he escaped and arrived home to my mother with a very recently killed hen clamped in his jaws, feathers flying, and bearing in mind that our house backed onto farmland where sheep were grazed, she was left with only one option: Sooty would have to go. But where? As dog lovers, euthanasia was not appealing, but the story of the murdered hen had spread like wildfire, and nobody in the neighbourhood would touch him with a barge pole.

At this point, Gerald introduced us to his cousin Peter, a delightful, kind, down-to-earth farmer, who wanted a dog for round the place, and said if he killed a hen or two, it wouldn't be the end of the world. So Sooty became a farm dog and, finding plenty of wide-open spaces to run off his not inconsiderable energy, never killed a living thing again. He even adopted a lame hen as his companion in the farmyard! He also paid his debt to his rescuer. Peter was awakened from sleep one night by a furious barking, and emerged from his room to discover that the dog had cornered a burglar on the landing, and such was the sight of his stripped fangs and the rumble of his growl, that the man was relieved when Peter called the police.

The upshot of this was that Peter in his turn became a firm friend, another admirer of Mona's, and a frequent visitor – a rival in Gerald's eyes. Tolerable; but only just.

About a year after Peter came into our lives, Gerald came in one night with the news that a local construction firm was looking for a wood machinist, my father's

——— ∞ ———

job, at which he was employed in Dublin, coming home at weekends. This was a golden opportunity for him and he applied for, and was offered the job soon after.

Grateful as he was for the news of the job, my father did not encourage the nocturnal visits, and soon these began to taper off, finally ceasing altogether. It was then that the poison-pen letters started. I never knew what they contained, but I remember my mother's distress, and two things which made me really afraid. My mother was confiding in a good friend and neighbour, Tommy, and she expressed her intention of going to Gerald's house to confront him and demand that he stop what he was doing. Tommy's reaction was immediate:

"Promise me that you will do nothing of the kind, or that if you do, you'll take a man with you. That boy's dangerous."

In the event Peter went. He confronted Gerald with some of his more virulent letters and told him he was liable to be charged with libel.

"You know these are complete lies," he said, "You can't say anything about that family, everyone knows they are above reproach."

He banged his fist on the table and stared into Peter's face.

"I didn't say I could say it; I said I would say it."

In the end, solicitors were brought in, and our acquaintance with the Doctor reached its perhaps inevitable end.

But there's so much good in the worst of us.

My prized possession as a child was a malformed

teddy bear called Rupert, named after Rupert Davis whom I watched weekly in the television serialisation of Simenon's *Maigret* – not who you thought! He was spotted on the farthest shelf of a shop belonging to my mother's friend Violet McCrory, where he had probably languished for years as in all the best stories. He was probably hand-made, of coarse grey woollen fabric, with little stick-like arms and legs and such a sad face that my mother stitched on a smile with pink wool, but my heart was his entirely. While my pals paraded their prettiest dolls in their prams and Tan-sads, I wheeled Rupert and bore with fortitude the slings and arrows hurled at him by insensitive adults and children who judged everything by appearance.

One evening, after a particularly biting criticism of my favourite, I came into the house close to tears. There was Gerald, in the midst of some deep philosophical discourse, but he paused to ask me,

"Is something the matter?"

"It's Rupert," I said, "Everybody laughs at him."

"You must admit," put in my mother, "He's remarkably ugly."

"May I see him?" asked Doctor Who.

I removed him from the pram, thinking what's one insult more or less? Gerald examined the exhibit for some moments in solemn silence. I held my breath. At last he handed him back to me.

"He has a very intelligent profile," he observed.

Perhaps I found the good that night.

———— ✺ ————

EPILOGUE

Gerald passed out of our lives and we heard little of him for years, but that little confirmed that he continued in his eccentric ways. Several other families bore the brunt of his spleen and, before the end of his life, he was totally friendless.

His sister Mae was as odd as he was, but very good-natured. A great lover of dogs, she worked tirelessly for their welfare through a number of charities. She was an ardent admirer of mine and cherished an ambition to marry me off to a young doctor of her acquaintance, but I was an unwilling partner in this enterprise, so it never came to fruition!

She lived to a ripe old age and was pre-deceased by the Doctor.

My father was one of the few people who attended his funeral.

Quoth the Raven

When I was a child, I did not know whether we were rich or poor; it simply never occurred to me. We had plenty of food to eat, always a good fire in the grate, nice clothes to wear with a special outfit for Sunday, and that was all we needed. We didn't have a telephone or a car, but neither did any of my friends; we did not go on foreign holidays, but neither did anyone I knew. We had as much as our neighbours and we were content.

But I had something extra for which I have had cause to be grateful many a time since – I had a family whose greatest pleasure was storytelling, and a mother who had a gift for setting the scene and creating an atmosphere that some of today's high-flying interior designers would kill for. A good friend recalls her first visit to our house thus:

> *"We came downstairs to the basement kitchen and were met by the sight of a roaring fire, in front of which was a thick red hearth rug reflecting the fire-light. On a table in the corner was a small lamp with a red shade, casting a cosy glow over the pro-ceedings. Coats were taken, chairs drawn up to the fire, and soon there was crack and presently a wee drop of tea, more yarns, and maybe a wee run of the cards. It was a different world."*

We had a television from about 1960, but in our house it was turned on to watch a carefully selected programme and then turned off – not for us the background noise and constant flicker that has been the death-knell of the art of conversation in so many houses. If we weren't telling yarns we were making them up; we used to choose a topic, say the first paragraph of a Victorian romance, and we would all write a sample. These would be read out and discussed and the best one chosen; the winner got to choose the next topic. We wrote reams of dog-gerel verse, about any event that happened in the town, such as the blowing up of the TA camp at the top of The Square, or Mona's departure to England for a holi-day, a tradition I have maintained, penning the ode for my parents' Ruby Wedding party as well as many events that happen at work. But above all we read poetry.

There was almost no type of verse that we did not like except the modern kind that is really prose masquerading as the real thing, and our favourites were anything that dealt with the supernatural. *The Ballad of the Little Black Hound, The Listeners* and of course *The Raven*, all had the power to raise the hairs on arms and necks and send delicious little frissons down the spine. Even now the recollection of Mona's sibilant rendition of

Once upon a midnight dreary, while I pondered weak and weary,
Over many a quaint and curious volume of forgotten lore...

has me reaching for a sweater.

This penchant for the macabre was more than the ordinary person's love of being frightened within the safety of their own four walls, for ghosts had always played an important part in my family's history. There was a time when we were all closer to the spirit world than we are now, or it was closer to us. Were we less sophisticated and more gullible? Or less arrogant and more open to the existence of otherness? Looking out tonight at the first snow of winter, watching it inexorably cover up grass, fields, roads and trees, wrapping everything in its own peculiar silence, it is easy to imagine a more innocent world with no mobile phones or faxes, no e-mails or internet to make a mockery of distance, a world in which the afterlife was just around the corner, and those who had gone before us had not gone far.

The house I was brought up in was in the middle of an Edwardian terrace, three storeys high at the back because of a cellar and two at the front. That it was haunted was accepted by all as a simple matter of fact. Many different people over a span of years saw a man in a brown suit pass through rooms where he had no business to be. My uncle felt the bedclothes pulled clear off the bed one night, and saw the man in the suit standing at the foot of the bed watching him. My godmother was awakened by the crying of her new-born daughter who lay in a cot beside the bed; horrified to see what she took to be an intruder standing over her, she immediately lifted the baby into her own bed; the man disappeared. My mother and Mona one night lay in bed chatting and giggling as girls do, and heard footsteps approach and enter the room. Assuming it was their brother Charlie come to chastise them, they were immediately silent; the man in the suit passed through their room unspeaking. Many a time throughout my childhood I lay and listened to steady footsteps coming up the stairs and crossing the landing, but no one was there. I was neither afraid nor curious; they were as much a part of the house as the drip of a tap or the creaking of the branches of the big tree outside my window. People in the other houses in the terrace saw the man many times, and the belief arose that he was the shade of the man who had built the houses in the first place.

The story goes that he had got into debt and was facing ruin when the bank foreclosed on his loans. The houses were offered for sale but no one would bid against the popular Felix except one man, who bought the twelve houses for a song. Felix's body was later recovered from the quarry.

If Felix's spirit did haunt the scene of his ruin, his was a melancholy rather than a frightening presence, but one incident from my mother's childhood was more disturbing. My grandfather, as I've said, had emigrated to the USA, to carve out a new life for his family, but before he could finalise arrangements he was struck down with a brain tumour and was admitted to hospital for treatment. Communication was not what it is now, and each day saw the family anxiously watching the post for news of his progress.

One night, my mother was in bed in the small back room she shared with Mona when suddenly the air was rent by a piercing shriek from the foot of the bed. My grandmother came rushing in to see what was the matter, but was assured by the terrified girls that neither one was responsible. Shaken, they all tried to settle back to sleep, but soon it came again, from the exact same spot. This time everyone, even young brother Wilf, asleep in an adjoining room, heard it. Sleep effectively banished, all four sat on the bed waiting for they knew not what, but the shriek was repeated a third time, and on this occasion the spaniel, Dash, came flying up the stairs two at a time as if the devil himself were after him, leapt onto the bed and lay growling at something at the foot of the bed *that only he could see*. Nothing more occurred during the night and eventually Dash was persuaded to go back downstairs and everyone settled down as best they could.

First thing in the morning, Mrs. Ritchie, the next-door neighbour, called at the door. My mother opened it.

"Are you alright?" asked Teesie. "Yes," replied my mother truthfully; she did not say they had not slept a wink.

"Are you *all* alright?" pursued Teesie. Again she was told, yes.

"Promise me you'll not tell your mother what I'm going to ask you next."

Puzzled, my mother agreed. "Last night," said Teesie, "me and Billy were wakened by the most awful shriek from your house, and we thought you must have got bad news, or that someone was dreadfully ill; but I wouldn't come in till this morning. Are you sure nothing happened?"

"Yes," answered my mother, now filled with foreboding, "We're all fine."

But the next day brought the news they had dreaded – my grandfather, having survived an operation to remove the tumour, had been sitting on the veranda in the hospital chatting to fellow patients, when he suffered a haemorrhage and died within minutes – at about the time the screams were heard.

Bad news travels fast, and soon the local curate, Fr. McGarvey, called to offer what comfort he could. My grandmother was not superstitious, but the incident troubled her and she confided in the priest. He said solemnly,

"Mrs. Campbell, your husband may have died in America, but his soul passed through here." And it may have done, for would not a man want to take a last farewell of those he loved in life?

My great-grandfather had a brush with the supernatural as a young man in Ballymulderg. He was a keen ploughman, who won many a medal in matches up and down the country, and one day he set out for Magherafelt to get a coulter repaired for the next big competition. The job took longer than expected and it was at a late hour that he found himself returning home, but many's the time he had walked it and he knew the road well. Suddenly another walker joined him and, though he did not know him, he was glad enough of the company to shorten the road. But his companion was taciturn and spoke not a word, even when John advised him to watch his step, for there was work being carried out at such and such a place, or to mind Keevins' dog, for it was famously cross. It was at this point that fear entered the equation, for the dog jumped the wall with its teeth stripped – *and jumped back cowering with its tail between its legs.* My great-grandfather had no option but to continue, but he did so a very scared young man. When he reached the part of the road known as Ned's Turn, his companion unaccountably vanished and he made the last part of his journey in a state of shock bordering on abject terror. He reached home soaked in sweat and with a fever on him which was to last many days. His cousin was then parish priest at The Loup, and he confided his experience to him, half-expecting it to be dismissed, but Fr. Larkin said,

"It may have been a troubled spirit who wanted you to do something for him, and they say that if you ask such a one in the name of God what they want, they must speak; but perhaps it is as well not to ask, for they may lay upon you a duty you would find hard to fulfil. I will say a Mass for him at least; and for you too."

Now John made a partial recovery, but was far from being the happy-go-lucky young man he had been and it was suggested that a spell by the sea might do him good, a favourite cure in those days, so he set out for Cushendun, accompanied by an aunt. One day as they sat on a bench enjoying the sights, they were joined by a man of indeterminate age but pleasant demeanour, who chatted to them in a desultory fashion for a while and then asked,

"Has the boy been ill?"

They assented, his aunt explaining, "He has suffered an unsettling experience and has not quite recovered from it."

The man drew from his pocket pen and paper and scribbled something upon it. "Take this to the chemist and ask him to make it up for you; you will find it will help."

Willing to try anything, his aunt obtained from the chemist a small bottle of medicine that John duly took, and within a few weeks was restored not only to health but also to spirits. His father had no doubt as to the efficacy of the stranger's remedy, and travelled to Cushendun to meet him and thank him for his timely intervention. But not a trace of the man was to be found in or around the village and no one could recall anyone of his description being there recently. Perhaps he was just a stranger in the right place at the right time, or perhaps he was, as my family believed, one and the same man who had accompanied John in so bizarre a fashion, and who may have been saying thank you for the prayers offered for his soul.

Another branch of the family had other reasons to respect the otherworld. At a gathering in another Larkin house around the turn of the century the crack was going well and everyone was in good fettle. Suddenly the sound was heard of a trap or similar conveyance approaching the front door, followed moments later by a loud knock. The man of the house rose to invite the newcomer to enter, but found to his amazement that the door would not open. Laughing at his weakness, several men went to assist him, but to no avail. At this his wife, upbraiding the folly of men, approached and opened the door at a touch; there was nothing there but darkness and silence. She was dead in the morning.

In my own lifetime, interest in ghosts was undiminished. I vividly recall the crowds of neighbours who went nightly to stand opposite the old Technical School on the Donaghmore Road, waiting for a glimpse of a spectral light which was said to have been seen by many a pedestrian on his way home late at night. I could not honestly say whether I saw anything or not, for there were so many cries of "There's it now!" or "Wheest! What's that?" that it would be hard to separate fancy from truth, but I know now that the school was built on the site of one of Bianconi's coaching inns, and that the legend 'stable yard' could still be seen around the arch above the side gate until the building was demolished sometime in the '70s, that decade of destruction. The main road as I knew it was like a 'Y' – the base was Ann Street and the right arm became the Donaghmore Road. But if you had taken the left fork you would have found yourself on the Gallows Hill which ran behind Hales's field, later the site of the new St Patrick's Girls' Intermediate School, and that was the way the coaches went after they had changed horses at the inn. Is it any wonder the residents of the Donaghmore Road and Ann Street were used to having their sleep disturbed by the sound of carriage wheels on many a crisp frosty night? No one I knew ever actually saw the headless coachman who was said to drive them, but the mere mention of his approach was enough to get the most recalcitrant toddler to bed.

And if you could have travelled as the crow flies from the Gallows Hill, you would have found yourself at the top of Beech Valley, formerly Windmill Hill, or to most of the locals, 'the winemill'. A story began to circulate in the early '50s that a ghostly figure had been seen on the hill, and again crowds flocked to see it. There were those who came to ghost hunt, while others came to scoff; some came with an open mind, some with derision; and some came for the crack. My family was in the latter camp, but with Mona aboard there was at least one person who fervently wanted to believe in the ghost, while just as fervently hoping not to see it.

Several nights were spent in fruitless standing about, and then the hunt was suspended, for Charlie and his wife Ann were expected home for the holidays with the children. But Ann expressed an interest in the tale and so another expedition was mounted, everyone setting off at dead of night full of the delicious excitement we usually experience when we watch a scary movie from the safety of our own fireside. The company comprised my mother, Mona, Charlie, Wilf, Ann and several friends, and they set off in high good humour. But when they got to the place there was a distinct feeling that all was not right. The atmosphere was palpably more sinister than on previous visits and there was a sense of malice in the air; but perhaps this was because the crowds were thinner tonight. The women linked arms and huddled together, talk fizzled out and everyone strained their eyes into the darkness looking for – what? Suddenly there was a noise like a stone clattering along a corrugated roof and an indistinguishable figure appeared for a moment on the skyline. The women felt a shiver of alarm, and then my mother said,

"Ach it's only the quarefella trying to frighten us!"

"It's not," said Wilf from directly behind her, more soberly than usual; "I haven't moved."

They all stood irresolute, everyone uncomfortable, and then Wilf said, "We'll split into two groups and meet up in fifteen minutes," and so they did. Comparing notes, they were all in agreement that nothing more untoward had been heard or seen, when suddenly Wilf gripped my mother's arm and cried out,

"There it, is, damn it, there it is!"

Again the women saw nothing, but suddenly Charlie said in a voice that brooked no contradiction,

"We'll go home, folks; this is no place for us here."

It was a sombre party that wended its way home, but in the warm kitchen where Granny was waiting with the teapot ready, it seemed frivolous enough, and the talk resumed, with only Charlie and Wilfred unduly quiet. At last Charlie said, "Tell me the truth boy, did you see anything?"

"I swear to God I did," said Wilf.

Charlie went off in search of pencil and paper. He gave a sheet to Wilf and said, "You draw what you saw and I'll draw what I saw."

After a few minutes, they compared their efforts. Now neither one was an artist, but like most people could make a stab at a basic shape, and they had each produced a creditable likeness of a robed and hooded figure.

There was no more talk about it and the ghost-hunting stopped, if only in deference to Charlie's having made everybody present promise faithfully never to go back to the Windmill Hill on such an errand.

As I grew up, I always retained a certain wariness of that site and did not like driving past it when years later Wilf returned from England to live nearby. When I discovered that wonderful repository of Dungannon lore,

Tyrone Precinct, I was intrigued to discover that in the time of the O'Neills' supremacy in Tyrone they established a number of monastic foundations, one of which was said to be at the top of the Windmill. Not one of my family knew that until then; but it's possible that they caught a whisper from a time long forgotten, an imprint on the very air of the place. We shall never know.

No one in my mother's family was ever afraid to die, which always struck me as odd, considering how much they loved life. But while not relishing the end of existence as they knew it, nonetheless they faced it stoically. Their attitude can best be summed up by one of my mother's favourite songs, sung with great skill and relish by the magnificent Tommy Makem, and with equal gusto if somewhat less skill by all of us, at some stage in every big night we ever had. 'Rosin the Bow', the aged fiddler, contemplates his death,

> *I've travelled all over this world,*
> *And now to another I go,*

and he makes robust arrangements for his wake, requesting plenty of drink, pretty girls to mourn him, stout fellows to bury him and even a hogshead of whiskey for the Devil himself, should he try to claim Rosin's soul. He finishes with,

> *I hear that old tyrant approaching.*
> *That cruel remorseless old foe,*

And I lift up my glass in his honour,
Take a drink with oul Rosin the bow!

I think their attitude was very much like Rosin's: Death was to be faced, not feared; they were going somewhere else; and they knew that someone would come to help them over the final threshold.

My grandmother Campbell died from stomach cancer after a lengthy illness throughout which she had suffered no pain, only a totally debilitating weakness that confined her to bed. As a result she was on no medication that could have dulled her senses or produced hallucinations. She lay in the small room off the sitting room, which was reached via the main door of the house. This arrangement allowed her many friends to come in and out to visit her without someone having to run up the stairs from the basement kitchen to answer the door, and all the neighbours availed of it. The usual pattern was that they would spend some time with her before coming on down for a chat with my mother or Mona; if they were pressed for time, they would shout a greeting down the stairs and go on about their business, so we were well used to comings and goings. One day as we sat in the kitchen we distinctly heard the front door open and a firm tread approach Granny's room. After a moment or two my mother said,

"That might be Wilf, I'll get the kettle on," for he was working locally and came home for lunch, always calling in with the patient before eating.

But then we heard the footsteps again, this time leaving the room and going out the door.

"Damn!" said mum. "I'll bet that was the doctor and I wanted to talk to him," and off she went up the stairs to see if she could catch him. As she passed Granny's room she called out,

"Did you have a visitor?" My grandmother told her, yes, but when mum got to the front door she found it locked. Puzzled, she returned to the bedside where she found Granny sitting up in bed smiling and happy, her eyes aglow.

"I thought you said you had a visitor?" began my mother.

"I had," assured Granny; "A strange man came to see me." *Strange to you but not to me*, she seemed to say.

"What man?" pursued mum.

"Och now, you wouldn't know him, Maureen," smiled Granny, with the smile of one nursing a delightful secret. "And by the way, I'm going home this week."

My mother was aghast, thinking that her mind was wandering and she thought herself in hospital.

"But you are at home, mother," she assured her.

Granny looked at her for a moment before saying softly,

"No, Maureen love, this was never my home; but I'm going home this week."

Shaking her head, my mother began to doubt herself and went again to check the door: there was no doubt about it; it was locked *with the key on the inside*.

On the following evening Granny quietly fell into a

sleep from which she did not awake, and on the Friday went home to Ballymulderg where her heart had been throughout all the years she had lived in Dungannon. And the man? We can only guess, but my grandmother adored her father, who had taught her to shoot, to love books and to be her own woman; and in the face of such a momentous event, we all need someone older and wiser.

As my uncle Charlie lay dying in Birmingham, he was privileged to have all his family around him. We used to congregate in his room every evening, for he still wanted to hear the crack and listen to stories and old well-loved poems. He looked over to where Mona sat, and said,

"Move over, like a good girl, till I see who that is behind you."

Automatically she complied, and Charlie thanked her with his grave courtesy and a wee smile on his lips. Seconds later, she realised there was no one behind her – *as far as she could see.*

My mother fought her own battle with cancer for a while and on the night she died, fought hardest of all, talking night-long about all manner of things as if determined not to be caught out by falling asleep. But Issy and I were with her in the side ward to which Dungannon's wonderful nurses had moved her when they realised it was only a matter of waiting, and we sat at the foot of her bed, now and then moistening her lips made dry by the oxygen mask. Suddenly we looked round as the door opened, expecting one of the nurses, but no one was there. A draught, we agreed. But mum looked up and said,

"So many of you here!" and then, "Mona? Mona! And Mama!"

After that she relaxed and seemed content and allowed herself to fall asleep.

Make what you like of these tales; I present them as I know them. There was a time when we accepted that a higher power was at work in the world, but now we believe we can rationalise anything, given long enough. Perhaps we can. But I think of Poe's Raven, *'from the Night's Plutonian shore,'* and I think about my forebears, who *were* less sophisticated and more gullible, but arguably the better for it. And I recall the sense of wonder a good ghost story could give you, with an odd reassurance in its tacit acceptance that life will continue elsewhere. I remember Frank Doran, friend of so many years, saying,

"Every night I leave your house, the hair biz standing on the back of my neck till I get into my own house!" and I find it sad that in time to come such wonder will have vanished.

Will it ever return? I hope so; but at the back of my mind I hear the voice of the Raven as it repeats its melancholy refrain:

Never - nevermore!

Swansong

On the sixteenth of February 1994, a day when crisp hoar frost covered roads, buildings and landscape in a coating of virginal white, I walked in the woods of Parkanaur near Dungannon, and my mother started to die. The process had actually begun a long time before that, no one knows when; whenever the first rogue cell became cancerous and began its horrible cycle of reproduction that would eventually make her bowel so unhealthy that it would cease to function normally, and her grip on life, once so determined, too weak to endure. But on this day the final hurdle was passed. She had been in hospital for less than two weeks, for she had only admitted to how ill she felt when it was too difficult for her to pretend any longer. They had removed a large section of her bowel and carried out a colostomy, with apparent success, but she had few resources to fight with. We discovered she was critically low in iron, had a heart defect, and she then fell prey to septicaemia, and finally to pneumonia. On this particular day, when I arrived for my visit, the nurses told me there had been a significant decline in her condition. When I approached her bed, she looked up at me and stated,

"I'm dying, love."

"Of course you're not," was my automatic response; but she glared at me as if to say *please don't treat me like an idiot* and reaffirmed,

"Ach, but I am, Aideen."

There was nothing to say to that, so I asked her,

"Are you frightened?"

"No!" she assured me.

"Well then," I said; and we chatted on about inconsequential things as if we hadn't just looked the greatest mystery of life straight in the face and passed on.

It was that night the nurses moved her into a side ward and we stayed with her until the end. It gave us a chance to look back on the year just past, which had been in so many ways one of the best years of her life, fittingly, since it was to be her last. It had begun with myself, Issy, her sister Marie and Mum, deciding to take a holiday house somewhere in the South, and spend a girls' week of sightseeing and crack, just us and the dog. Various combinations of friends and family had been doing these 'Southern holidays' for years, and we always had a ball, staying in Galway, Kerry, Wexford,

Waterford, Tipperary and so on. Our only criteria were that the house should have a good heating system and take dogs. This year, for reasons that escape me, we pitched on Leitrim. Now, bearing in mind that the pleasure of being away from home on holiday usually doubles in direct proportion to the distance you have to travel to reach your destination; and that for my mother the drive was as much a part of the holiday as the arrival, this was odd, to say the least. Odder still was the fact that usually we spent ages plotting our route and ETA and selecting several likely-looking pit-stops en route, while this year we simply climbed into the car and set off. Our consternation when, after a mere ninety minutes of driving, it became obvious that our destination was within spitting distance, was comical. We girls were prepared to be slightly amused; my mother was aghast. This was the sort of drive we did on a Sunday afternoon while my dad caught up on his sleep while pretending to read the Sunday papers, or after work on a summer's evening when we frequently drove away up beyond Omagh to walk Gollum in some obscure and well-hidden forest park. And yet here we were for our annual holiday! What was to be done? Needless to say Maureen was not going home, so we decided to make the best of it. We duly arrived at the house where we were met by the owner and her mother, two delightful people who decided there and then that if we had travelled such a short distance for our holiday, we must be unused to getting out much, so the mother immediately offered to take my mother shopping to Enniskillen the day after next! On a bus!! Unknown to this good lady, we had spent the previous Saturday in Enniskillen, and anyone who knows the road from Dungannon to the west will know that it's an easy run and one which we did many a time.

"The oul' eejit," remarked Maureen scathingly when they had gone; "Does she think I was never out before?"

We refrained from pointing out that in terms of age there wasn't much between them; but as I noted elsewhere, age was an acquaintance my mother refused to acknowledge.

"It's only talk," we said, "She'll not think of it again."

But as with many unpropitious starts, the holiday turned out to be one of our best ever. The crack was mighty; the house comfortable; the scenery wonderful; the weather good. There was plenty to see and do, no men to bother us with demands for papers, news, regular meals and decent hours. We could sit up until three a.m. and stay in bed till noon; and often did. Sometimes we skipped lunch to finish a scenic drive and assuaged our hunger with crisps and chocolate bars eaten in the car; Maureen, ensconced in the front seat, would hold the driver's Coke can and pass it over when required. She enjoyed these impromptu picnics as much as any seven-year-old.

The funniest incident was the arrival, on the Tuesday morning, of mine hostess at the door, ready for the road.

"Is the old lady ready yet?" she enquired of Marie, who opened the door.

I was helping my mother get ready, for the early-morning stiffness caused by her chronic arthritis made dressing and hair-arranging a chore. Marie came in with the news that the bus was waiting for her up the road. Nothing would persuade Maureen that this was not a fabrication of Marie's 'for badness', till a skelly out revealed the other woman waiting for her. Then the laughter began, and it was with difficulty that we managed to convey her regrets that due to her state of unreadiness, she would have to forgo the pleasure of the trip. The rest of the holiday was punctuated with gales of merriment at the idea that Maureen would go shopping to Enniskillen (on a bus!) with a bunch of old women, "and me only there last week."

"Still, it was nice of her to think of it," she would try to be just. "But girls" – squeals of mirth – "can't you just see me?"

One of the most enduring cameos of my mother, for me, comes from this holiday. We stopped off at the Slieve Russell Hotel near Cavan town, known, so a Dublin taxi driver told us, as 'the Jaysus hotel'. Why? Because there's nothing for miles around and suddenly you come on this enormous edifice that would look more at home on a film set for *Gone With the Wind*, and all you can say is 'Jaysus!'

We, at any rate, decided to take afternoon tea there. Marie, Issy and I were in Barbours and jeans, because we had the task of walking the dog, and as all dog own-ers know, mud and dog hairs don't sit comfortably on pencil skirts and sheer tights. My mother, on the other hand, looked like an ad for *Country Life*. She was attired in a smart navy blazer, pristine white shirt and straight skirt; her hair for once was immaculate and her skin had a glow from being out in the fresh air that made her look far younger than her years. She carried her cane with the brass dog's head and, while we fell on the food with an appetite sharpened by our dog-walk, she leant on this cane, sipped tea and smoked with the aplomb of Bette Davis. Perched on a straight-backed chair while we slumped in sofas, she regaled us with tales of her youth, her past loves, her friendships, while we sat mesmerised by this doyenne of taletellers. I can still call this vignette to mind vividly, the cosy fire in the grate, the evening drawing in, the indifferent food forgotten as she wove her spell. I do not know how long we sat there fascinated. I only know that we agreed among ourselves later that we could have stayed forever.

Another highlight of this last twelvemonth was our trip to Dublin. We had promised to take her to Dublin for her birthday and to do it in style, so the Famous Four booked into The Gresham, forgetting that the date we chose was the weekend of the All-Ireland Gaelic football semi-final. But as luck would have it, one of the semi-finalists that year was Derry, my mother's home county and, as even better luck would have it, Derry won. The hotel had been block-booked by Derry supporters and the atmosphere that Saturday evening was electric. Everyone was happy, everyone sang, everyone was at peace with his neighbour, even the Dubliners, for in my experience Gaelic followers are great sportsmen, and

———— ∞ ————

there was no ill-will anywhere. My mother was beaming, as if somehow her presence there had influenced the result. As we came through the foyer after dinner, she leant over a tableful of Derry fans, total strangers to her of course, and murmured,

"Well done! I'm a county-woman of yours, you know."

A young man jumped up and swung her round in an enthusiastic embrace, accompanied by cheers from his companions. It made her day.

The following day, we took her for a ride around Dublin in a hansom cab. She sat up like the Queen and waved with great solemnity at everyone she passed, occasionally inclining her head if someone caught her eye or returned her salute.

"Girls," she told us, "I missed my vocation; this is what I was born to do."

That weekend also she had enjoyed her food with an appetite that she had not displayed for many a day. It is easy to recognise with hindsight that her dramatic loss of appetite was a direct result of the cancer that was slowly but surely sapping her life force, but at the time I told her she was picky, fussy, not interested in food, or just too fond of talking to stop and eat. But in The Gresham she made a fine trencherman, sending us back to the excellent buffet at breakfast time for second helpings of tiny cocktail sausages and toast, and in the evenings, always choosing with relish from the extensive menu. One night she was awakened by nausea, and we put it down to over-indulgence, kidding her along about high living. We never do heed the warning signs; but then again, as she always said, "It's a veil of mercy that hides the future from us." Would we have been so happy on that autumn weekend in Dublin if we had known we would never do it again? But we did not know, and it was just another episode in a year of wonderful episodes –

But the true highlight of the year was The Party …

... To End All Parties

My mother, Maureen Brigid Campbell, met my father, Patrick Joseph D'Arcy, in Birmingham, in 1952. He was my uncle Charlie's best friend and had been much talked of on Charlie's visits home. It became the standing joke in our house that Maureen would go on a visit and sweep this poor unsuspecting chap off his feet, luring him back to the wee black north where they would make a man of him.

"He'll meet his Waterloo when he meets me," she avowed, little believing that her prophecy would indeed come true.

They married in Dungannon in 1953 and went to live

in Birmingham, but finding themselves one year later the proud parents of their first and only child, they relocated to Maureen's home town, influenced, perhaps, by Wilf's scathing assessment of Birmingham:

"I wouldn't rare a cat in this hole."

I only realised when reading through her correspondence after her death that she and Albert Jehoulet, the Belgian doctor who, she always affirmed, was the love of her youth, actually kept in contact until just before she got to know my father. Sadly, the correspondence has huge gaps in it, and I have no idea if the relationship was broken off after Maureen and Pat became acquainted, or if she and Albert had agreed to part before my dad came on the scene. She never said; and for many years I thought the talk of Albert was a smokescreen for her true feelings, for Maureen was never one to wear her heart on her sleeve. She even found it difficult to tell me she loved me, and I know that she loved me above anything else on this earth. The nearest she came to it was the Christmas before she died. She had bought me a book of love poetry by women entitled *Love's Witness*, and on the flyleaf she had inscribed:

To Aideen, who has always been a great love's witness for me. From Mum (Not always).

I wept when she gave it to me, that this woman, who loved to describe herself as 'a tough nut,' and 'a hardy annual', who above all things eschewed displays of emotion and thought herself hard, could, in this one message, convey a lifetime's awareness of the bittersweet and often difficult relationship that exists between mother and daughter, and it touched me at the deep heart's core. If she can see me now, I'll bet she's saying,

"Sure you should have known I was on my way out; I wouldn't have written that if I was going to be around much longer."

So I will never know the truth of the Maureen-Albert-Patrick scenario and guesswork is futile. I used to wish she had married Albert, because I thought it would be romantic to be half-Belgian; now of course I know that had she done so, I would have been an entirely different person and would probably have had romantic notions of life in Ireland; but you don't know that at seven.

My father was born in 1925 in the small village of Passage East, a picture-postcard village on the Suir estuary, seven miles from Waterford city, and mercifully protected from commercialisation by its proximity to Tramore and Dunmore East. He was the son of Margaret (Cis) Sheeran and Tom D'Arcy, who was in the merchant navy. Almost all the families in the village made their living from the sea, mostly by fishing. There were a few exceptions, like the schoolmaster or the postmistress, but ninety-nine people out of a hundred owed their living to the grey widow-maker, and a hard taskmistress she was. My grandmother's close friend, Nellie Gunnip, lost five brothers to the sea, and in my lifetime, it claimed her only son, Eddie. Bountiful it may be, but as the sea gives, so does it take. It yields its harvest and it takes its toll. But always it casts its spell. I love the sea, and whether I have inherited this love from my father or from my Cancerian star-sign I don't know. But I love its colours, its moods and its music; its smell and its unpredictability enchant me. I don't swim, but I love beaches, the warm sand or the cool shingle and always the susurration and the sound of the waves. My mother, on the other hand, was a landlubber, tolerating the sea only because the rest of us loved it, and staying inland whenever she could.

My mother and father had almost nothing in common and I suspect that their mutual attraction owed something to the esteem in which each was held by Charlie, who was an object of admiration for them both. But they had a long and outwardly happy marriage, which gave me a stable and love-filled childhood, in which my father fell easily into a supporting role for the much more sociable Maureen. He had his own tales to tell, but he did not share her skill as a teller, nor her enjoyment in the part; and many people never heard his tales, at least until they got to know him very well.

My father was solid, reliable and undemanding, a regular and unambitious worker who was in many respects married to his work. He refused to come to my graduation ceremony because it would have necessitated taking time off. Needless to say, more than ten years after his retirement the firm is as busy as ever, its profit margins growing all the time. To my mother, nothing was more important than family occasions; Hell and high water were minor distractions where such things were concerned. She treasured family lore, whereas my dad could never see why relatives should interest him, and would have found it hard to name four of his cousins. She was outgoing, he was not; my dad loved ballroom dancing, Maureen saw a dance as an opportunity to catch up on crack. My mother had a wicked sense of humour, while my dad's lacked subtlety; but most of all, he was no match for Maureen intellectually, and he constantly dwelt in her shadow.

I recognise now that both partners were dissatisfied, if not disappointed. My mother grew to love my dad as a partner will, but she was never in love with him, as I think he was with her. If I had tried to discuss their relationship I know I would have been fended off with persiflage and quizzing jocularity; she would not have revealed anything of her true feelings, but often, as she herself would have said, there's many a true word spoken in jest, and I believe her throwaway asides about Albert being her soul mate contained more than a grain of that most elusive truth. Among all the letters that she kept, very few are from admirers, being mostly family documents; the ones that are, are from Albert. Once, moved by an instinct we did not understand, she showed us a lock of his hair. Oddly enough, when going through her things after her death, it was nowhere to be seen.

However that may be, my parents remained steadfastly married for more than forty years, and I believe in the end they were both content. He was a good provider, she never wanted for anything and, if sometimes she wondered about an alternative scenario, she kept it to herself.

———— ❧ ————

In the thirty-ninth year of their marriage, Issy and I went to stay in London with my cousin Mo whose own marriage had broken up, and she was in that period of uncertainty in which she was trying to believe that she and her partner would get back together, while at the same time, beginning to plan for life on her own. I have always been a regular church-goer, Mo not, but she always came with me and on the Sunday morning we headed off, leaving Issy at home with the two Jack Russells, Dandy and Jezebel. When we came back, we found her busily engaged on a thorough spring-clean of the kitchen, merrily mopping the floor, dishes cleared, worktops shining.

"My God!" exclaimed Mo. "What's all this?"

"Haven't you ever heard of the Immaculate Reception?" enquired Issy.

I should explain here that Mo is the daughter of my uncle Charlie, and therefore my first cousin and my mother's niece and namesake, for years being distinguished as Wee Maureen, later as Young Maureen and finally, as Little Mo. She is seven years my senior and in many ways, more like my mother than I am. When my mother and father were first married, Young Maureen was like a daughter to them, staying at weekends, being taken to the pictures, told stories and all that I would later share in. She and my mother had a very close and special relationship, and shared the same talent for mimicry and story telling, and the same wit and humour. They understood each other's foibles and loved each other in spite of them.

On this particular occasion, Issy's comment had us in stitches and set the mood for the rest of the day. We were determined to be happy, the sun was shining and the future seemed not so bad. We poured the wine and switched on the radio and sang along... and then they played The Song.

The Song has been in my family for years, trotted out at the drop of any hat, on all occasions and, as with almost everything in my family, it has a Story attached to it.

One day my grandmother answered a knock at the door, to find thereat a woman (and several of her brood!) who declared that she had just moved to Dungannon and had sought Granny out because they were related. The lady was Mrs. Murray, the only woman who ever caused me to cry as a baby, for I was a placid child and smiled obligingly at everyone who peeped into my carrycot until Mrs. Murray attempted the move and I screamed blue murder, refusing to desist until Annie Wadsworth, a sensible soul, intervened and elbowed her out of the way, dangling a set of keys at me. It was widely supposed that her trilling laugh was what did the damage; my mother nicknamed her 'Lady Ha-Ha'. I do not recall the incident myself, but like many of the stories I grew up with, I have heard it so often that I almost begin to believe that I do.

As it turned out, she and my family were not related at all, or at least very tenuously, she having a cousin married to a cousin of my grandmother's, but it was enough to encourage her to claim kinship, and insist upon her visiting rights. She adored the odour of sanctity and, since my grandmother had several cousins who had answered the call to become men of the cloth, she cultivated the friendship carefully, perhaps hoping some of their virtue would rub off on her.

"I don't know why," remarked Maureen one day. "They never did me any good."

This was true, for as a pupil at St Patrick's Girls' Academy she and her pal Shona were often in trouble for talking and even smoking, and one of the nuns told her she had seven devils in her; and this without knowing that the flowers she had presented to Reverend Mother in an effort to deflect her wrath at their returning late from lunch on still another occasion, had been culled en route from the nuns' own garden. Still, when some years later the nuns presented her to a visiting missionary sister as a possible candidate for convent life, and Maureen reminded Mother Kevin of the seven devils, the nun twinkled at her.

"But they were seven good devils, Maureen alannah."

It was Mrs. Murray's elder daughter Gracie who introduced The Song. She regarded herself as a soprano of worth, and consequently always treated any company she happened to be in to a recital. Everyone knows someone who expects to be asked to sing at a social gathering, but Gracie differed in one respect – she did not wait to be asked. It was her custom to take up position on one side of the fire and, during a lull in the conversation, launch into song. She favoured ballads rich in pathos, such as

—— ∞ ——

High on the belfry the old sexton stands,
Grasping the rope with his thin bony hands

or sentimental ditties like

There's a grey lock or two in the brown of your hair;
There's some silver in mine, too, I see.

This last one she sang with great feeling, giving heart-felt sighs and pregnant pauses between phrases for effect; so much so that Wilf said "you could slip out and make the tay while Gracie was murdering a daycent song."

But her pièce de résistance was The Song, which always ended the recital, and its accompaniment was Gracie tapping her large feet ("that would trip a train" according to Maureen), and poking the fire in time to the rhythm. Not infrequently, she poked the fire out. Granny tried many ruses to secrete the implement out of Gracie's reach, but with the unerring instinct of a homing pigeon, she would fasten upon it wherever it reposed in time for the rendition. It went as follows:

There once was a Jew and he lived in Jerusalem,
Glory Hallelujah, old Rogerum.
He wore a tweed cap and a scarf round his neckium,
Glory Hallelujah, old Rogerum.
Skinnymalink madoodium, glory Hallelujah,
Glory Hallelujah, old Rogerum.

The good man died and he went up to Heavenium,

Glory Hallelujah, old Rogerum;
He had breakfast with the saints at a quarter past elev-
enium,
Glory Hallelujah, old Rogerum.

The bad man died and he went down to Hellium,
Glory Hallelujah, old Rogerum
He was shovelling coal with the oul' black Divilium,
Glory Hallelujah, old Rogerum.

So thanks be to God we are all stoneybrokium,
Glory Hallelujah, old Rogerum;
Skinnymalink madoodium, Glory Hallelujah,
Glory Hallelujah, old Rogerum.

This always reduced us to giggling wrecks, but not before we had lustily sung every line of it, and on this occasion it prompted a flood of 'D'ye minds' from Mo and me about life on the Donaghmore Road and episodes from our childhood, and somewhere among these came the realisation that mum and dad would be married forty years the following July. Then and there the preparation for The Party began.[3]

When I die, be it sooner or later, I reckon I will not be remembered for much, and that's fine by me; but I know I will be remembered for a time at least for

---

3. Oddly , it was a rendition of this song by Len Graham and John Campbell at a story-telling course we attended that persuaded Issy and I to write these memoirs. It provoked a good deal of discussion as to provenance and origin, as well as much mirth; and reminded us again just what a storehouse of humour my mother was. Oh, and by the way, it's based on the Bible story of Dives and Lazarus; but you knew that, didn't you?

being involved in one of the best parties Dungannon ever witnessed. Issy and I put heart and soul into it and everybody connected with it gave it their all. First and foremost, it was to be a surprise. Although my mother was a party animal, she had been complaining for some time about 'oul' wind pains', a symptom of the cancer, had we but known it and she was suffering greatly from arthritis, which curtailed her enjoyment of social functions, and also inhibited her from looking her best, since she could no longer wear the smart shoes which, because of her excellent legs, had always been her trademark. We knew, therefore, that had we suggested a party, she would have vetoed it, so instead we talked about a nice meal out. All the guests were sworn to secrecy and so close did they keep it, that two best friends, who met every evening in life for a walk and a chinwag, were amazed to see each other there on the appointed night!

We secured a room in the recently refurbished Dunowen Inn and set up a range of display boards covered with newspaper cuttings, including the wedding pictures, photographs and '50s memorabilia, so that early arrivals would have plenty to talk about. We trawled everywhere to secure bits and bobs to add to the ambience – a sculpture of an elderly couple to adorn the specially commissioned cake; a silver loving cup for the couple to drink the toast; a hand-blocked book from Wales, for all the guests to sign; and the anniversary gift from Issy and myself – a pair of gold Claddagh wedding rings, inside which we had inscribed *Fide et Amore* – By Faith and By Love. Maureen always said she was married on a curtain ring, for slender bands were in vogue in the '50s, and my dad had never had a ring, for the fashion for men to wear wedding bands had not yet arrived, so the idea was a big hit. The blessing of the rings halfway through the evening by my mother's cousin Fr. Vincent Darragh was the only solemn moment in a night of unmitigated joy and fun; and even the seriousness of that was lightened by Maureen's asides as the poor priest sought to do the thing right.

We had agreed that I would leave the house early, ostensibly to collect Wilf and then come back for mum and dad; but in reality, we had arranged for another friend, Eamon, to collect them in a limousine and drive them slowly around the town en route to the venue. Teresa Fahy, whose family has been friends with ours for many years, had suggested that her fiancé should video the proceedings; I at first demurred, for my mother hated photographs, but finally assented for I knew it would be a lovely memento. And so, as they left the house, they caught a glimpse of Joseph deftly wielding the camcorder from the cover of a nearby hedge. At this point, mum had realised that something was afoot, while Patrick, as usual, was several steps behind. When Eamon dropped them off at The Dunowen, I was waiting to greet them, attired in a '20s style cocktail dress with a silver filet and black feathers in my hair, sheer black tights and stiletto heels, though I had left the house in a raincoat. All this passed my dad by.

"There was some guy with a camera outside our gate," he informed me with deep suspicion. "And what happened to your car? Did you have an accident? Why didn't you come back for us?"

I can still see my mother rolling her eyes and saying,

"Ach, shut up Pat and follow Diamond Lil."

(As it turned out, Maureen adored the video and watched it time and time again with unalloyed delight.)

The whole evening was conducted along the lines of a wedding, by a master of ceremonies without equal, our great friend and inimitable character, Martin Fahy, though Maureen even managed to upstage him. She was on sparkling form and never sat down the whole evening, flitting from table to table as she recognised old friends she had not seen for many years and talking to them all. What struck us about the gathering that night was the palpable goodwill you felt as you entered the room; there were cousins, friends old and new, neighbours and family; but they were united by two things: their love and respect for this woman; and their determination to have a ball. We had engaged the services of a couple of chaps to provide music for us and I remember saying to Gregory,

"Play it by ear; if no one dances, play some background stuff."

For I was thinking that the majority of the company was past retirement age, but I needn't have worried. The floor was full all night, from the first note to the last. The men, like the gentlemen they were, made sure that every lady had a partner. Even Maureen was persuaded to dance by Frank Doran, by what magic, I will never know. Towards the end of the night, while the younger ones were recovering on the soft seats around the room, the old ones were still going strong. While Gregory enjoyed a rest, Paulette slipped out and donned her grass-skirt, cycling shorts and mask and gave us a hysterical send-up of a kissogram; Little Mo murdered *Dirty Old Town*, while Patsy sang (and danced) *The Sash* and got halfway through *Wee Hughie*, before forgetting the words. Martin kept the ball rolling all night, whether by producing the outfit my dad wore on his wedding night (an empty hanger) or asking my mum what she wore, unprepared for her swift response,

"Chanel No. 5."

And he read aloud the ode I had penned in an attempt to acknowledge all the good friends we had made down all the days and at the end we drank a toast to absent friends. Now when I read the poem and see just how many are gone from us, I see that evening as something of a bonus, a night for everyone to celebrate what it is to have a friend and to be one.

One who was absent on the night was Dessie, son of my dad's good friend Vinnie, and like a son to Maureen and Pat himself. Like many another good man, he liked a drink, and so he absented himself from the festivities in case he would get carried away and overdo it. (He needn't have worried; Uncle Wilf held on manfully for most of the night but eventually was caught just before he fell off a chair and was surreptitiously slipped home by Frank Doran, Issy and myself before anyone noticed).

But Dessie turned up at the house the following night

to convey his best wishes and entertain us with his own brand of humour.

"Did I ever tell you about yer man taking me, as a wee fella, to the football match? At half time, he went and bought us both a slider. When we had licked all the ice cream out and the wafers were almost touching, he turns to me and says, 'Hi, boy! Do ye ate the two wee boords as well?'"

"Hi Pat, d'ye mind the boy who used to work with us in Monaghan – the Orangeman? I met him at the Twelfth in Benburb a wheen o' years ago."

"What were you doing at the Twelfth, Des?"

"Me and the boys had got a load of strawberries and we went out to sell them. I know they mightn't 'a' bought them if they had known we were the other side, but right enough, yer man never let on. He just bought his strawberries, give us a wink and went on."

Dessie was a tradesman of great skill, a joiner to trade but adept at many things, and I never saw anyone who could work so fast. It was while he was engaged in putting up a fence in our back garden that he died, a victim of a massive heart attack at forty-nine years of age. Mum rang me to my place of work to tell me of the tragedy, and my first thought was that it simply couldn't be true; my second was, what a waste – so much to offer the world, so young to leave it. It is my firm belief that the shock of his death and the trauma of having to wait while first the paramedics, then the doctor and finally the police came and did whatever had to be done, greatly accelerated the spread of the cancer in my mother;

and I saw something die in my dad that day too, for Dessie was greatly loved by us all. Recently I was speaking to Issy about Death and I said,

"Why is it that good people die and people like so-and-so live on?" and she offered a very original piece of philosophy.

"Maybe God just gets bored and needs people like your mum to give him a bit of crack."

He would get plenty from Dessie.

When we finally got home from the party in the small hours and squeezed everybody who was staying in the house into some sort of sleeping apparatus, Issy and I crawled into a tiny single bed, top and tail, to seek a well-earned rest. Suddenly, the door opened and there stood Maureen, wreathed in smiles, completely unabashed at the time (going on for five a.m.) or the fact that we had been on the go from about the same time the day before, for all the transport of goods, chattels and people, fell to us; and oblivious that, now that the months of planning had finally come to fruition, there comes the lassitude that follows on the adrenaline rush of achievement. She was, as I say, beaming, and wielding the inevitable cigarette.

"I just wanted to thank you girls for my party," she announced. "You know I'm not good at saying thanks, but…"

We were too tired to realise it at the time, but her words encapsulated much that I have tried to rationalise about my mum and dad's relationship. It was very definitely *her* party. People who came were *her* friends in the main, who liked or admired my dad and saw him as a good man, but their love was for her, and they knew that where she was, there would be crack and laughter and a drop of tay. He was incidental to her, and though she protected and shielded him and would have defended him from the criticism of others, she always knew this. Watching her work her way around that room, I was watching a solo effort. He smiled and chatted in response to others; she was the instigator. She was pleased if he was happy, but her happiness did not depend upon his. They were complementary, but never co-dependent. Later I found that Issy had picked up on this as well. Hindsight is a gift; or maybe not.

"Did you enjoy yourself?" I think I mumbled.

"I did surely; and what's more, I never had pain or ache all night!"

This was by way of being a small miracle, for later we knew that she had lived with pain for many months.

It was as she finally left the room that she uttered the words that have warmed and amused us many a time since.

"And you know, Issy, I love you as much as I love Aideen there, you're my number two daughter."

Then she considered what she had said and, forced into complete accuracy by her sense of well being and happiness, she amended,

"Well, maybe I love her just a wee bit more."

∞

Did you ever, in your life, have an idea that you think would please someone you love, and you don't carry it through, for whatever reason? I've done it many times, but on this occasion, harassed by Issy and greatly assisted by her, I stuck with it. When mum died, Annie Bunting came to her wake.

"I met a woman on the way down here," she told me, "and she asked me was I at That Party. Was I at That Party? I said. You can bet your life I was and I never had as good a night in my life. And everybody else thought so too."

That's what made us glad we did it. So go for it!

EPILOGUE

During the writing of this memoir, my dad was diagnosed as a victim of Alzheimer's disease, a condition which in the early stages rendered him unable to concentrate on reading, or to understand what he read, and so robbed him of one of his greatest pleasures. Like the parasite that it is, it has continued to destroy all the things that made him what he was – his dignity; the strength that made him so firm a reference point for us all; his knowledge of who he is, and all the myriad little things that make each of us unique. It has left him his quiet courtesy, his fortitude and his sense of humour, even though we none of us can share in the laughter any more. One devastating effect is that he no longer recognises me, his only child, once the focus of all his care and attention and also, sometimes, a source of pride.

Another is that he was unable to read this book in preparation and enjoy the shared memories, and will never read it now. But he's still a part of all that I am, all that Maureen was, and our debt of love and gratitude to him is immense. I hope that somewhere, deep in the recesses of a mind now closed to normal communication, he knows this.

APPENDIX I

Verse and Worse

My grandfather's closest friend in his youth and early manhood was his cousin Tommy Duffin, with whom he exchanged many letters in verse. Sadly, only one of these has survived, but it's an interesting one in that it describes a journey home from Ballymulderg to Kilsally by bicycle, after a night's ceilidh, and mentions some of the families we knew so well.

The Pilgrim's Progress

When Watersons had gone to bed
And Milligans by instinct led
Had followed Nature's Law, and fed,
And then to rest themselves betaken,
With the first sign of day to waken,
I thought that it was time to go
Although it was but twelve or so.
I therefore rose and said "Good Bye,
"The moon yet glimmers in the sky,
"A desperate man to take my flight,
"Agin the law, without a light."
I took my old velocipede,
My fastest friend in time of speed,
Each circling tube I did inflate
With air pumped up at rapid rate,
And when upon the highway free,

LIE OVER DA

—— ∞ ——

I said 'So long' to Wilfred C.
My foot upon the paddle flung
As lightly to the seat I sprung,
And from the anti-torrid North
I went for all that I was worth.
Past Foster's gate, and Quigley's too,
Impelled by midnight fear I flew.
The hedges rustled eerily,
The wind was moaning drearily.
And worst of all when down each slope
I gave my double-wheeler 'rope'
When I began to tramp once more,
Round whirled the 'paddles' with a snore;
But only for a time; the ratch-
-Et freed again began to catch.
And then in trepidation, lest
'Twould fail again if left unprest,
I paddled down each long declivity,
Thinking on all my past depravity,
Lest that I should, by force of gravity,
Hit the hard road in fierce collision
Through some mechanical omission.

'Twere long to tell, to trace 'twere hard
Each step twixt Loup and Druminard,
Where Atty Thra's descendants still
Exist on Ballynuey Hill.
But free and fast as cyclone blast
O'er stone and waterpool I passed.
Down that precipitous descent,

Fear with exhilaration blent,
Unbraked and unpropelled I went.
But gathered force of motion failed
Ere Ruskey Hill I had assailed,
And where the roads transversal cross,
Amid that spent and wasted 'moss',
Alas, 'twas useless to complain,
I had perforce to tramp again.

An eerie shudder shook the night,
A faint and wavering haze of light
Broke thro' the frontal prospect far,
As the dim light of clouded star,
Clearer it grew and yet more clear,
The sound came stronger on the ear,
And up the hill and o'er its crest
(A load was lifted from my breast)
Twin stars of flame shone fierce and far:
The headlights of a motor car,
Expanding as they nearer came,
They almost merged in common flame
It passed me with a roar and flare
And petrol fume that filled the air.
With saddened gaze I turned away,
And mused, 'Will e'er I see the day
'When at my pleasure I can board
'My Mercedes, Darracq, or Ford?
'And ride for pleasure or for gain?'
Alas, I fear the wish is vain.
Such written musings dew the eye

Of those who read, in sympathy.
On through the night without a light
I strained my unrelaxing sight,
Lest objects in the road should lie,
Which, if observed, I might slip by,
Such as a man with whiskey sated,
In other words, inebriated,
Or whitethorn bush with barb like wire
To puncture a pneumatic tyre.
Alas, my friend, I'll have to stop,
Of ink I haven't left a drop,
My fingers weary with the strain,
Although as much and more again
I could indite to gratify
Your high-arch-super-critic's eye.
But now I'll have to whittle short
The story of my further sport.
I passed by Tamlaght's Synagogue,
I went like blazes past Cloghog -
-Al's ponderous Druidical stone,
At that dread hour of night alone!
Then Coagh by moonlight I surveyed,
A calm reposeful scene it made,
'Twas like a city of the dead
Whence all domestic life has fled.
Light I observed not, gleam nor spark,
The very dogs forbore to bark.

I stood in Coagh, upon Hanover Street,
A public house and barracks on each hand;

I saw no bobby on his midnight beat,
Nor heard him say, in tones of stern command,
'Without a light the law you dare to cheat!
'Name and address deliver, where you stand!'
Because they all were sunk in sweet repose,
In calm oblivion of friends or foes,
A fleet of Zeppelins underneath their nose
Had winged their way (that's rather low, I s'pose)
And left unruffled their complacent doze.

Perceiving that the coast was clear,
I barely could repress a cheer,
Reaching the corner of the Square,
I turned in that direction, where
Lies Coagh's Whitechapel and Soho,
Appropriately named 'Red Row'.
The denizens were all asleep,
I saw no desperadoes creep
Becloaked and masked, on murder bent,
Or with burglarious intent.
But halt! I must abbreviate,
And plainly and unvarnished state,
That I went out the Urbal way,
And onward thence through Aughavey.
I passed that house of stone and brick,
Where Wallace Sam, the lunatic,
With Bible, gun, and blackthorn stick,
Played many a wild and savage trick -
The fruits of his unbalanced mind -
But now he's cabin'd, cribb'd, confined,

A sad example unto those
Who can't keep on sufficient clothes.
At length Kilsally's bounds I passed
And reached my journey's end at last.
So farewell paper, ink, and pen,
When I affix my cognomen…

The Author, TJD

PS. I hope you are alright yoursel',
And all the others too, as well;
Old folks and young, both M and B,
And Mr. Charlie Patrick C.

TJD.

The last line fixes the date somewhere before 1920, since Charlie is the only child mentioned and the rest were born after this time. 'M' is my grandmother, Minnie, 'B' her sister Brigid.

My mother's first job was in a hairdressing salon owned by Mrs. Agnew, in Hanover Square, in Coagh (I don't think the Duffin connection had anything to do with this!). She always told me that when St. Patrick was making his way around Ireland he came one day to that village, pausing for a moment to view it, and take its measure. After a moment, he remarked, 'Coagh, you're there,' and moved on. It hadn't changed much in her day, which probably accounts for the boredom which drove her and her workmates to try their hand at versifying. Freddie O'Dee was from Tipperary, Lily McKee from Ballinderry, whence she cycled each day, and they intended to immortalise their customers in their rhyme.

Mind you, not every member of staff was of such a literary bent. Maureen had one apprentice who kept disappearing out the back during working hours and one day mum's curiosity got the better of her. She found her charge practising Irish dancing in an outhouse. Maureen promptly advised her to make up her mind on her choice of career, since, she affirmed, she could train her to dress hair, but would not, though she could, under-

take a Terpsichorean role. It was shortly after this that Mum opened her own business in Dungannon.

'Twas in the month of sweet July that first to Coagh we came,
And since that happy summer day the place has gained its fame;
With lifting faces, cutting nails, and curling hair all day,
The pass-word here is 'Glamour' - at least that's what they say.

Now business soon was flourishing, I hereby do declare,
And all the ladies came in crowds to see about their hair;
But soon a cloud o'ershadowed it, which made the neighbours stare,
As one by one they slithered past 'Salon Hanover Square'.

What wrought this transformation we never have found out,

But something here has gone amiss, that goes without a doubt;
We've smiled and scowled alternately; in fact, we've even bowed.
But history will repeat itself, for that we have allowed.

Our clientele was varied, the truth I must confess;
Some said we made them beautiful; some just assented, 'Yes'.
Some certainly had hearts of gold and weren't hard to please;
But some odd folks, I'll guarantee, would shake you at the knees.

First came Mrs. Daly, always bright and gay;
She still gives us her custom, as also does Miss Grey;
And then we have 'The Mrs. Brown', who lives just over there,
But she is very finicky about her long straight hair.

Now Mrs. Duff and Mrs. George are not so hard to please,
The former always pleasant, the latter likes to tease.
And then we have the Miss McVeys, a cheeky lot are they,
They always come at half-past eight - though they're at home all day.

The parson's wife I can't describe, perverse she likes to be,
When Maureen smiles, 'A lovely day,' 'Oh, nonsense, child,' says she.
She also has another fault, in that she's very near;
She never purchased anything; 'twas always 'far too dear'.

There is a Miss Gillespie, a daughter of her nibs,
The bones are almost sticking out through all her blooming ribs;
She ain't as bad as mother, the truth we have to tell;
But who is this just coming in? My God! It's Mrs. Bell!

From Drumard House this pest arrives, to be contrary she contrives,

———— ∞ ————

Her accent? It is just a lisp; her hair? A lank and greasy wisp;
In hubby and in Baby Bess a feigned interest we profess,
But what we say when she has gone, I'll leave that for you folk to guess.

Our social callers here are few; of course in Coagh they're all true blue,
But up Main Street lives 'Greasy Balls', and late at night she always calls;
Miss Sheehy lives across the way; she sure will come, but will she pay?
Her hair is tinted brown with tea; we don't get much by her, you see.

In Coagh town are two cobblers, McGrath and Liam McCombs,
If you favour one with custom, you should hear the other's groans.
And then come Mrs. Flack and Hugh; we'll give them still a point or two,
But of that crowd they're still the best, and we have put them to the test.

Now when some months had passed away, to this salon there came one day
All ready with white coat and fee, a smart young lass called Miss McKee,
To learn the trade she was inclined, and so the pact was duly signed,
Assisted by this expert pair, she's got the art of fixing hair.

Apparently she liked the place, for soon appeared another face,
A shy and modest little lassie, and soon we learned her name was Cassie;
Now both these girls are very good, but like ourselves they miss their food,
It's tea and toast, and toast and tea - please take that stuff away from me!

Now to continue with our song, we really won't detain you long;
A few more words about the boss, and do not ask me 'Is she cross?'
In Dublin Freddie sealed her fate; alas, she found it out too late.
And for her love of fixing hair, she's planted in Hanover Square.

You've heard our troubles; are they few? We cannot say, we're asking you;

But when the darkest cloud hangs o'er, our sense of humour's to the fore,
And on the darkest, dullest day, we still succeed in feeling gay;
Our pass-word now is 'We don't care! We still must stick Hanover
Square.'

Now to conclude this rambling rhyme, we fear we've taken up your time;
Duty calls; we have to go, to meet again our hairy foe.
Although we must admit with sorrow, it's hair today and gone tomorrow;
However, we will do our best, and hope the hair will stand the test.

Dungannon, Tip, and Ballinderry; we hope you folk can feel as merry,
And if you want to get your fella, just drop in here and get a Wella;
The darkest clouds are silver-lined, at least so say the undersigned.

Here comes the bus, we must get ready, good luck and love,
Maureen and Freddie.

Written and composed by above, on this 6th day of June, in
the year 1949.

They certainly believed in doing it in the grand style
and for once, Maureen did not try to obliterate the date.

My aunt Mona was famous for her tidiness and house-
pride. The following ditty was penned in the '50s when
she went to Birmingham to spend some time with brother Charlie, his wife Ann and the two children, Maureen
and Margaret. Frank was one of her admirers, Seamus

was Barney's son, of whom more later, Barry was really Charlie Colfer but we always called him Barry because of his likeness to Barry Fitzgerald. Larry was a Dungannon man in temporary residence in Birmingham, whose habit of reading aloud from the evening paper drove everyone to distraction, especially when he produced gems such as, "So and so was married today; it says here the bride carried a bucket of white carnations." At least she was original.

Dear Mona,

Ever since you went away everything has gone astray.
The food is poison, germs are ramp, and even Frank
has taken cramp. The dishes are not washed all
day, the Mater's hair is turning grey; the clothes are
always in the tub, and Wilf is yelling for his grub.

The dogs are daily growing thinner, for as you know
they get no dinner; they look at Maureen and seem
to whisper, 'for goodness' sake, bring back your sister!'

The house is wretched, cold and dark; as for the fire,
there's not a spark; a neat ghost walks from room to
room - Be God! It's Mona with her broom.

Dungannon's still upon the hill, there's some folks
dying and some folks ill; some like Seamus go away,
but what d'ye know, return next day. Poor Phillie
cried and said 'Good-bye! Oh! hurry back, or I'll

*sure die.' But Seamus said 'Now Phillie dear, I won't
be long, so never fear.' And sure enough, he came
next day - the work in England didn't pay; and then
what did this bold man do? He signed once more on
the old 'buroo'.*

*In upper Ann Street late last night, M. Cullen got
an awful fright – as she opened up the door she
found Frank Loughran on the floor, and in his hand
he clutched a card, his breath was coming very hard.
She said 'What ails you, Frankie dear? You know my
husband sleeps in here!' Then Frankie rose up like a
man, the word he murmured low was – 'Ann! Why
did you take my girl away and have me going on
this way?'*

*There's something I would like to know, how are
you getting on, dear Mo? How are the kids? How is
dear Ann? And have you got yourself a man? As you
know, there's no excuse, with Mick Devine still running loose; and then you have the charming Barry,
and don't forget our old friend Larry. But! Mona
Dear, keep this in mind – remember those you left
behind.*

*The folks all here are missing you (you must excuse
a lie or two). This letter, dear, I now must end, I'll
still remain your loving friend.*

Mick Devine was a friend whose parents had left

Donegal for Scotland when Mick was only a baby. Consequently, he spoke with a thick Glaswegian accent, but was aggressively Irish. He always had to be asked to sing, and his party piece was *The Flower of Sweet Strabane*, sung through clenched teeth and with a pronounced nasal drawl. One night he, Charlie and Wilf were in a pub in Birmingham, and Mick started to sing *Johnson's Motor Car*, a somewhat Republican ballad, and suddenly a row erupted between the locals and the large Irish contingent at the bar. Mick, who was tiny, retreated under a table where he finished his recital, while punches flew all around him.

Seamus, Barney's son, was renowned for his total and absolute aversion to work. Such was his antipathy, that when his first son was born, Frank Loughran told my mother he was to be called Brian Boro. Wilf and Charlie found this reluctance hard to believe, and became convinced that it was only lack of opportunity which held Seamus back; consequently, they and some friends got together and found him a job in Birmingham, arranged digs and his passage over, and congratulated themselves on a job well done. He lasted a month and mum received this letter from Wilf telling her the news. Anyone familiar with the works of Robert Service will catch more than a passing echo.

This is the song of Barney's son,

As he squats in his digs alone,
On the wild weird nights when the electric lights
Shoot up from the Gladstone Road.

I'm one of the Dungannon bureau boys,
I'm an old time pioneer;
I came last month - oh! God how I've cursed
This Birmingham - but still I'm here.

I've tried my best in this Devil's land
Where I've played, and I've lost, the game;
An ordinary guy with a craze for dough
But never a cent to my name.

This working is only a gamble,
The worst is as good as the best,
I was in with the bunch and I might have come out
Right there on top with the rest.

With D'Arcy, Campbell, and Anderson -
Oh God! But it's hell to think
That I might have stopped at home on the dole
And had money for cards and drink.

Money was just like dirt there,
Easy to get and to spend.
I sure was set on staying on,
But they got me a job in the end.

It put me queer, and for part of a year

I could hardly draw my breath,
Till I found myself in Birmingham -
It looks like being my death.

Four long weeks in Birmingham,
Struggling along its streets,
Roaming its dreadful factories -
It sure gives me the creeps.

Tired and weak, but no matter,
There's dole in Dungannon still;
I'll pack up my things tomorrow,
And hop on the boat to Phil.

Wilf's comment is, "I think it's not much fun for Barney's son."

The last offering in this section is my own and I include it in the form in which it was presented to everyone who came to mum and dad's Ruby Wedding party. It was intended as a tribute to all our good friends, as well as a bit of fun; it still is.

The Toast of '53

There was a wee lassie called Maureen
Who lived on the Donaghmore Road;
She owned a hair-dressing salon

⎯⎯⎯ ∞ ⎯⎯⎯

Where the cream of Dungannon would go
To be Marcel-waved, coiffeured, and curlered,
And manicured, fingers and toes:
Says Maureen, 'Send in your oul' nettles;
I'll turn each one out like a rose.'

Then she heard that her brother in England
Had a close bosom friend, name of 'Pat';
And they told her he hadn't a girlfriend,
Says Maureen, 'We'll soon settle that.'
So she upped and she travelled to England
Via Belfast to Heysham all night;
And she got poor oul' Pat all bewildered,
And says he, 'She's a smasher, all right.'

He was charmed by her northern attraction;
He just didn't know what to do;
Says Maureen, 'I told everybody
When we met I'd be his Waterloo.'
Very soon they were planning a wedding,
In Dungannon, that place of renown,
And Mo's brother, the quarefella Wilfred,
Says 'That'll cost me forty pound,
To ensure that there's plenty of whiskey
To help poor oul' Pat keep his nerve;
For you know, he's a right sort of craythur,
Which is more than the oul' girl deserves!'

Undismayed by the awful occurrence
When the Princess Victoria went down,

Maureen travelled home the next evening
To be married in her old home town.
In Dungannon they did not long linger,
But as soon as the wedding was done
They set off via Dublin for Passage
To meet the D'Arcy clan, every one.

Once again they set sail for old England,
In Birmingham town they did dwell,
And many's the yarn and the story
That Maureen's relations could tell
Of the exploits and jollifications
Between Margaret, and Frank, and young Mo,
And the recently married young couple,
In their flat, Number 1, Claremont Road.

But one day, says Maureen to Patrick,
'It's time back to Ireland we went,
For I have to inform you, dear husband,
We're expecting a happy event.'
And so it was just one year later
That the two were augmented to three,
And when Pat heard the child was a daughter,
He said, 'Well, no Ford Mustang for me!'

Once again they returned to Dungannon;
The crack was as good as before,
And all the old friends were as faithful
As they ever had been heretofore.

There was Kathleen, who, up at the corner,
Was keeping the neighbourhood shop,
Where all kinds of goods and provisions
Could be purchased, all at one stop;
And as well as the eggs and the bacon,
The bread and the milk and the tay,
There was news, views, and gossip, and stories,
From morning till midnight, all day.

Maureen joined with the Musical Society
To pass long winter evenings away,
And the Company's production of 'Show Boat'
Is still being talked of today.
You have only to mention 'Dahomey'
To Patsy or Seamus McKeown,
And you'll see their eyes growing all misty
As the memories flood back, one by one.

And Pat would go up of an evening
And take a wee walk round the town,
And it might be in Charlie McKenna's,
Or over in Doran's he'd be found.
And Maureen looked up all her old friends,
But not being contented with that
Said 'We'll widen our circle of acquaintance.'
'There's safety in numbers,' says Pat.

So all through the years they're together
Not a single occasion was missed
When the tiniest chance has arisen

To add more new friends to the list.
So a health to the new and the old friends,
Who have proved themselves time after time,
Far too many to list in this saga –
How the hell could I get them to rhyme?
So to Donnellys, and Hamills and Maddens,
Fahys, Mooneys, and Raffertys too;
To Joan, Gerald, and Sybil and Evelyn,
And to Luttons and Quinns, not a few;
To O'Connells, and Corrigans, and Campbells,
Friends and relatives, all of good will,
And the many who sadly are absent,
But who live in our memories still;
To Johnstons, O'Neills, and to Buntings,
To Hugheses and Dalys and all,
To Swifts and McCurrys and Loughrans,
We hope that you all have a ball!

And as we are gathered together,
Looking back over years that have gone,
When between us we all have experiences
Sadness, joy, heartbreak, laughter, and fun;
I hope we remember the good times,
And forget disappointments and tears,
As we join in a toast – TO THE COUPLE!
And here's to the next forty years!

APPENDIX II

Snapshots

Maureen Campbell in typical Carmen Miranda mode with sister-in-law Ann, nieces Margaret (front L) and wee Maureen (front R) and Ann's niece, Barbara

Mary Josephine Larkin, daughter of John Larkin and Britta Smyth

Patrick Joseph D'Arcy was a keen ballroom dancer – an interest not shared by his wife, who regarded time not spent talking as time wasted!

Maureen won many prizes for singing; note the altered date on this one!

Wilfred Campbell, whose emigration to America changed many lives and many destinies

The Laconia, *the ship on which Wilfred Campbell sailed to America*

Jamaica, Long Island, New York, the area which became his home

Ballymulderg:
Brigid, Mary Larkin's sister

Her son Dan

Annie and James Johnston, lifelong friends

Brigadier General Sean Larkin

Captain John L Smyth, a cousin of Mary Larkin. Killed at Gettysburg in 1863

Sgt John Vray, US Army 1944, who wanted to take Mona back to his ranch in Texas

Belgian René Dubois, young idealistic conscript who hated war

Sgt Ernest Price, the love of Mona's life who was tragically killed in Korea

A card from Albert, the doctor whom Maureen loved before she met Patrick D'Arcy. She kept a lock of his hair until the day she died. The hand-written message reads: "At the occurring of a nice voyage during which I thought very much to you", *signed by Albert and dated 7/12/1948*

Donaghmore Road days: good neighbours Alice and Francie McGeary

*Maureen in her hairdressing
days (L) with colleagues Lily
and Freddie*

*Minnie Larkin with granddaughter
Aideen in her beautiful cottage garden.
She said her only regret in dying lay in
not seeing Aideen growing up*

*Mary Larkin, cousin of Minnie
Larkin, victim of a bad marriage*

L to R: Charlie, Patrick D'Arcy's cousin Tom Sheeran and Tom Campbell outside the Imperial Hotel in Portadown (now Super-Valu!) where Maureen and Patrick held their wedding reception. It was Tom with whom Minnie Larkin entered into the ill-fated business venture that brought her to Dungannon

Patrick D'Arcy as a toddler; boys were often dressed as girls to confuse the fairies who might otherwise have stolen them away

Minnie Larkin, Mrs. Campbell, with Dash, the dog who heard the Banshee

Maureen and Aideen with a cousin, Dan Campbell

Mona in Thomas Street, Dungannon c.1958

Dear Reader

I hope you have enjoyed this publication from Ballyhay Books.
It is one of a growing number of local interest books published
under this imprint including Hugh Robinson's *Back Across
the Fields of Yesterday* and *The Book of 1000 Beautiful Things
and Other Favourites* : Viv Gotto's *Footprints in the Sand:* John
O'Sullivan's *Belfast City Hospital, a Photographic History* and
Harry Allen's *The Men of the Ards.*

To see details of these books as well as the beautifully illustrated
books of our sister imprint, Cottage Publications, why not visit
our website at **www.cottage-publications.com** or contact us at:–

Laurel Cottage
15 Ballyhay Rd
Donaghadee
Co. Down
N. Ireland
BT21 0NG

Tel: +44 (0)28 9188 8033

Timothy & Johnston

BALLYHAY BOOKS